Introducing Tom Wayman

Books by TOM WAYMAN

Waiting for Wayman
For and Against the Moon: Blues, Yells and Chuckles
Money and Rain: Tom Wayman Live!
Free Time
Living on the Ground: Tom Wayman Country

Edited:
Beaton Abbot's Got the Contract
A Government Job at Last
Going for Coffee

Ontario Review Press
Poetry Series

Introducing Tom Wayman

Selected Poems 1973-80

THE ONTARIO REVIEW PRESS
Princeton, New Jersey

Cover: photo by G.B. Henderson

Library of Congress Cataloging in Publication Data

Wayman, Thomas Ethan, 1945-
  Introducing Tom Wayman.

    (Ontario Review Press poetry series)
    I. Title   II. Series: Ontario Review Press.
Ontario Review Press poetry series.
PR199.3.W39A17   1980   811'.54   80-20260
ISBN 0-86538-003-1
ISBN 0-86538-004-X (pbk.)

Distributed by PERSEA BOOKS, Inc.
225 Lafayette Street
New York, N.Y. 10012

ACKNOWLEDGMENTS

I would like to thank especially Raymond J. Smith and Joyce Carol Oates for their encouragement, for the idea of this book, and for their selection of the poems. Poems here were first published in or accepted for: *Saturday Night, New: American and Canadian Poetry, The Ontario Review, The Lamp in the Spine, kayak, The Minnesota Review, The Fiddlehead, The Canadian Forum, This Magazine, Quarry, The Times Literary Supplement, Mainline, The Little Magazine, Repository, Queen's Quarterly, Copperfield, Sound Heritage, San José Studies, NeWest ReView, Canadian Literature, The Tamarack Review, Poetry Northwest, The American Review, Praxis, It Needs To Be Said, Northern Journey, Pebble, Grain, Concerning Poetry, Cafeteria.* These poems subsequently appeared in five collections of my work published in Canada by McClelland and Stewart Limited and The Macmillan Company of Canada Limited between 1973 and 1980.

"Days: Construction," "Unemployment," "Poem Composed in Rogue River Park, etc.," "Wayman in Love" from *Waiting for Wayman* and "Friday Night in Early September at Morris and Sara Wayman's Farm, Roseneath, Ontario," "Thinning Carrots," "Travelling Companions," "Metric Conversion," "Garrison," "The Calf," "The Whitewood Elegies," "Looking for Owls," "Egg City," "Teething," "Exploratory," "How Quiet," "Discomfort," "Tidewater," "Figuring," "Farewell to Wheeler Without Saying Goodbye," "La Lluvia de Tu Muerte," "An Epitaph: D.W.," "What Good Poems Are For" from *Living on the Ground: Tom Wayman Country* reprinted by permission of The Canadian Publishers, McClelland and Stewart Limited, Toronto.

"Garrison" was awarded first prize (The Holly Drew Geary Cooper Award) in the 1976 U.S. National Bicentennial Poetry Awards competition sponsored by the City of San José, California, and San José State University. Judges were Kathleen Fraser, Robert Hass, and Josephine Miles. The poem "The Death of Pablo Neruda" is based on a translation made for me by my uncle, Alexander Wayman, of an interview with Neruda's widow published in the *revista de revistas* of the Mexico City daily *Excelsior*, June 5, 1974. The title of my "La Lluvia de Tu Muerte" is a phrase from Neruda's poem "Alberto Rojas Jiménez viene volando."

I am grateful to Lorene Wilson for her assistance to this project. As this is the first book-length collection of my poems to appear in the U.S., I want to express my appreciation as well to American friends and teachers, among them Stuart Peterfreund, James B. Hall, James McMichael, Charles Wright, Nicholas Crome, Robert Bly, X.J. Kennedy and, always, John Woods.

And this is for: *Dennis Saleh.*

CONTENTS

LOOKING FOR OWLS

INDUSTRIAL MUSIC

DAYS: CONSTRUCTION

Days when the work does not end.
When the bath at home is like
cleaning another tool of the owner's.
A tool which functions better with the dust gone from its pores.
So that tomorrow the beads of sweat
can break out again along trouser-legs and sleeves.

And then bed. Night. The framing continues
inside the head: hammers pound on
through the resting brain. With each blow
the nails sink in, inch by blasted inch.
Now one bends, breaking the rhythm.
Creaks as it's tugged free. A new spike
is pounded in.

The ears ring with it. In the dark
this is the room where construction is.
Blow by blow, the studding goes up.
The joists are levered into place.
The hammers rise.

UNEMPLOYMENT

The chrome lid of the coffee pot
twists off, and the glass knob rinsed.
Lift out the assembly, dump
the grounds out. Wash the pot and
fill with water, put everything back with
fresh grounds and snap the top down.
Plug in again and wait.

Unemployment is also
a great snow deep around the house
choking the street, and the City.
Nothing moves. Newspaper photographs
show the traffic backed up for miles.
Going out to shovel the walk
I think how in a few days the sun will clear this.
No one will know I worked here.

This is like whatever I do.
How strange that so magnificent a thing as a body
with its twinges, its aches
should have all that chemistry, that bulk
the intricate electrical brain
subjected to something as tiny
as buying a postage stamp.
Or selling it.

Or waiting.

WAYMAN IN THE WORKFORCE:
ACTIVELY SEEKING EMPLOYMENT

Everybody was very nice. Each place Wayman went
the receptionist said: "Certainly we are hiring.
Just fill out one of these forms." Then, silence.
Wayman would call back each plant and corporation
and his telephone would explain: "Well, you see,
we do our hiring pretty much at random. Our interviewers
draw someone out of the stack of applications we have on file.
There's no telling when you might be notified: could be next week
or the week after that. Or, you might never hear from us at all."

One Thursday afternoon, Wayman's luck ran out.
He had just completed a form for a motor truck
manufacturing establishment, handed it in to the switchboard operator
and was headed happily out. "Just a minute, sir," the girl said.
"Please take a seat over there. Someone will see you about this."

Wayman's heart sank. He heard her dialling Personnel.
"There's a guy here willing to work full time
and he says he'll do anything," she said excitedly.
Around the corner strode a man in a suit. "Want a job, eh?" he said.
He initialled one corner of the application and left.
Then a man in a white coat appeared. "I'm Gerry," the newcomer said.
"This way." And he was gone through a doorway into the plant.

"We make seven trucks a day," Gerry shouted
standing sure-footedly amid a clanking, howling, bustling din.
"Over here is the cab shop, where you'll work. I'll be your foreman.
And here is the chassis assembly..." a speeding forklift narrowly
    missed them
"...and this is where we make the parts."
"Wait a minute," Wayman protested, his voice barely audible
above the roar of hammers, drills, and the rivet guns. "I'm pretty green
at this sort of thing."
                    "Nothing to worry about," Gerry said.
"Can you start tomorrow? Monday? Okay,
you enter through this door. I'll meet you here."
They were standing near an office marked *First Aid.*
"We have to do a minor physical on you now," Gerry said.
"Just step inside. I'll see you Monday."

5

Wayman went shakily in through the First Aid office doors.
"I need your medical history," the attendant said
as Wayman explained who he was. "Stand over here.
Thank you. Now drop your pants."
Wayman did as he was told. "You seem sort of nervous to me,"
the aid man said, as he wrote down notes to himself.
"Me, I'm a bit of an amateur psychologist. There are five hundred men
in this plant, and I know 'em all.
Got to, in my job. You shouldn't be nervous.
Remember when you apply for work you're really selling yourself.
Be bold. Where are you placed? Cab shop?
Nothing to worry about working there: monkey see, monkey do."

Then Wayman was pronounced fit, and the aid man escorted him
back through the roaring maze into the calm offices of Personnel.
There Wayman had to sign for time cards, employee number, health
    scheme
and only just managed to decline
company credit union, company insurance plan, and a company social
    club.
At last he was released, and found himself back on the street
clutching his new company parking lot sticker in a light rain.
Even in his slightly dazed condition,
a weekend away from actually starting work, Wayman could tell
he had just been hired.

THE FACTORY HOUR

The sun up through a blue mist
draws its own tide: this is the factory hour.
As I drive east, I pass dozens like myself
waiting on the curb for buses, for company crummies,
for car pools; grey plastic lunch buckets,
safety boots, old clothes. All of us pulled
on the same factory tide.

                       The plant's parking lot
is the dock; the small van of the industrial caterers
has opened at the furthest gate through the fence: coffee, cigarettes,
sandwiches. Walking in through the asphalt yard
we enter the hull of the vessel.

The great hold is readying itself for the voyage. Steam
rises slowly from the acid cleaning tanks
near the small parts conveyor and spray booth.
We pass to the racks of cards; sudden clang of machine shears
but otherwise only the hum of voices, generators, compressors.
Click and thump of the cards at the clock. The slow movement
of those already changed into blue coveralls.

The hooter sounds, and we're cast off. First coughs
and the mutter of the forklift engines.
Then the first rivets shot home in the cab shop's metal line.
Air hoses everywhere connected, beginning to hiss, the whir
of the hood line's drills. The first bolts are tightened:
the ship underway on the water of time.

Howl of the routers: smell of fiberglass dust.
Noise of the suction vacuum, the cutter, the roar
of dollies trundled in for a finished hood. And the PA endlessly calling
for partsmen, for foremen, for chargehands:
Neil Watt to Receiving please, Neil Watt.
Jeff Adamanchuck to Sheet Metal.
Dave Giberson to Gear Shop...to Parts Desk...Sub-Assembly.

The hooters marking the half-hours, the breaks,
the ship plunging ahead. The PA sounding

7

Call 1 for the superintendent; *Call 273; Call guardhouse; Call
    switchboard.*
Lunch at sea: sprawled by the hoods in ordinary weather
or outside at the doors to the parts-yard if fine; whine of the fans
and the constant shuttling of the forklifts
show that the ship still steams. Then the hooter
returns us back to the hours of eyebolts,
grilles, wiring headlamps, hoodguides, shaping and
sanding smooth the air-cleaner cutouts. On and on
under the whir of the half-ton crane, rattle of the impact wrench,
grating of new hood shells as they are dragged onto a pallet.

To the last note of the hooter: the boat returned to its City.
A final lineup at the timeclock, and out through the doors
to the dockside parking lot. Late afternoon:
I drive into the tide of homebound traffic, headed west now
still moving into the sun.

THE JIG

Andy and Bill are at work at the second station
of the fiberglass hood line: Andy is under the hood shell
that is fitted over the metal jig. The hood sits
as it will on the finished truck
but now with a man under it, not a motor.
Bill begins to drill holes in the shell
for lights and reflectors. Andy comes out for a moment and the two
hoist the radiator grille into place. Andy goes back inside.

Andy has worked here ten years. Before this he was a railroad switchman
in Canada and California. He did a term in the U.S. Army,
applied for citizenship but returned to Vancouver.
When he started here, the job began with a piece of sheet metal. Now
it's all assembly of parts formed elsewhere:
"like a giant Meccano set," he says. Six years ago
he got home from work to find his wife had left for Oregon
with his children. He went after them and discovered
his wife was in a mental institution, his children
placed in foster homes. He collected his kids and came back
but a social worker followed him north and convinced him
the children would be better off where they were.
Support money was wanted, though, and recently an Oregon county
has begun suing Andy. "Why should I send money?" Andy says.
"The kids won't get any of it. My ex-wife and the guy she lives with
are both real drunks, winos, and that's where the money will go.
When she left me, it took four years to pay off the debts
she'd run up. Now they want me to pay more.
It's like I'm being punished for something I didn't do."

Outside the hood Bill smokes his pipe
as he pushes through the bolts to hold the grille.
He is twenty-one, worked here five months.
He laughs cheerfully as Andy complains a bolt is too short.
"Angry Andy, Angry Andy," Bill says. No reply. Bill has been married
three months, and a first child is on the way.
Each coffee break and at lunch he is on the parts-desk phone to his wife.
"She's home alone in the apartment," he explains.
"It's only fair." Bill met his wife

9

a few months before they were married.
"I'd known her a long time earlier, though," he says.
"It's strange: I'd completely forgotten her. I'd been up
at Ashcroft for a year or two on a commune. When I got back
I met a friend who said she was in town again.
I couldn't remember who she was at first, but when I did
I said, 'Let's drive over and see her.' We did
and she had just broken up with her boyfriend or something.
Anyway, we went out together a few times and I knew
she was the one I wanted to marry."

He fondles his wrenches, screwdrivers, and ratchet, re-settling them
in his toolbox with his pipe and tobacco pouch.
"I knew she was the right one for me," Bill says seriously.
"I can't imagine ever going with anyone else."

Now he chuckles as Andy mutters something glum
out of the semi-darkness under the hood. Inside, Andy lifts
the impact wrench to the nuts he has fitted
as Bill outside puts his wrench to the head of each bolt.
For an instant as the nuts are tightened
the two are joined across fibreglass and metal.
What are they building this afternoon in their lives?
A 623 hood, marked for turnlights,
fender braces, grilledenser, and a large air-cleaner cutout.

FACTORY TIME

The day divides neatly into four parts
marked off by the breaks. The first quarter
is a full two hours, 7:30 to 9:30, but that's okay
in theory, because I'm supposed to be fresh, but in fact
after some evenings it's a long first two hours.
Then, a ten-minute break. Which is good
another way, too: the second quarter
thus has ten minutes knocked off, 9:40 to 11:30
which is only 110 minutes, or
to put it another way, if I look at my watch
and it says 11:10
I can cheer up because if I had still been in the first quarter
and had worked for 90 minutes there would be
30 minutes to go, but now there is only
20. If it had been the first quarter, I could expect
the same feeling at 9 o'clock as here I have
when it is already ten minutes after 11.

Then it's lunch: a stretch, and maybe a little walk around.
And at 12 sharp the endless quarter begins:
a full two afternoon hours. And it's only the start
of the afternoon. Nothing to hope for the whole time.
Come to think of it, today
is probably only Tuesday. Or worse, Monday,
with the week barely begun and the day
only just half over, four hours down
and 36 to go this week
(if the foreman doesn't come padding by about 3
some afternoon and ask us all to work overtime.)

Now while I'm trying to get through this early Tuesday afternoon
maybe this is a good place to say
Wednesday, Thursday and Friday have their personalities too.
As a matter of fact, Wednesday after lunch
I could be almost happy
because when that 12 noon hooter blast goes
the week is precisely and officially half over.
All downhill from here: Thursday, as you know
is the day before Friday
which means a little celebrating Thursday night

—perhaps a few rounds in the pub after supper—
won't do me any harm. If I don't get much sleep
Thursday night, so what? I can sleep in Saturday.
And Friday right after lunch Mike the foreman appears
with the long checks dripping out of his hands
and he is so polite to each of us as he passes them over
just like they taught him in foreman school.
After that, not too much gets done.
People go away into a corner and add and subtract like crazy
trying to catch the Company in a mistake
or figuring out what incredible percentage the government
has taken this week, or what the money will actually mean
in terms of savings or payments—and me, too.

But wait. It's still Tuesday afternoon.
And only the first half of that: all the minutes
until 2—which comes at last
and everyone drops what they are doing
if they hadn't already been drifting toward
their lunchboxes, or edging between the parts-racks
in the direction of the caterer's carts
which always appear a few minutes before the hooter
and may be taken on good authority as incontrovertible proof
that 2 o'clock is actually going to arrive.

And this last ten minute break of the day
is when I finally empty my lunchbox and the thermos inside
and put the now lightweight container back on its shelf
and dive into the day's fourth quarter: only 110 minutes.
Also, 20 to 30 minutes before the end I stop
and push a broom around, or just fiddle with something
or maybe fill up various parts-trays with washers
and bolts, or talk to the partsman, climb out of my
coveralls, and generally slack off.
Until the 4 p.m. hooter of hooters
when I dash to the timeclock, a little shoving and pushing
in line, and I'm done. Whew.

But even when I quit
the numbers of the minutes and hours from this shift
stick with me: I can look at a clock some morning
months afterwards, and see it is 20 minutes to 9

—that is, if I'm ever out of bed that early—
and the automatic computer in my head
starts to type out: *20 minutes to 9, that means*
30 minutes to work after 9: you are
50 minutes from the break; 50 minutes
of work, and it is only morning, and it is only
Monday, you poor dumb bastard....

And that's how it goes, round the clock, until a new time
from another job bores its way into my brain.

INVENTORY

Standing in the parts yard all day
in the heavy rain, rows of us
dressed in the cheap plastic dayglo hooded jackets
and waterproof pants the Company bought for
inventory, gloves soaked through
in the first twenty minutes of
reaching into the heavy wooden ring pallets
to pull out the dripping metal parts.

Larry and I began with steps: the metal beaded with rain,
water pouring out of the bent-in corners as
each step was lifted out to be counted: all the different ways
a man's foot can climb up onto a truck
with him not thinking for a second how
that step got there, formed from an expanded bar
of aluminum, or galvanized iron, given a certain number
in the factory where it was made, shipped to this place,
provided with another number that is stamped on it somewhere
and now, perhaps months or more than a year before anyone stands
    on it
the step gets taken out in the midst of a steady October downpour,
is counted and tossed back in
with somebody noting down its number and how many there are,
his sleeve dripping onto a damp card as he tries to write.

And the forklifts pass splashing through the maze of
pallets brought out into the aisles between the parts-racks
where wet figures in the bright orange plastic suits
bend over the contents—unidentified tubes, pipes, bars and castings
jumbled beside them—and others have climbed up ladders
and over the frames of the racks
to curse and keep counting in the endless rain.

Larry and I did mouldings next, and the following day
brackets, from massive metal plates to aluminum ones
so thin and tiny their assigned number
has to be hammered into wired-on metal tags
now lying nearly submerged in the puddles on their shelf.

Truck parts, in the rain. The water

14

soaking in at last through the stitching of my boots
as though I had hiked for hours down the mud
of a rainforest trail. In the woods: moss and ferns and the huge cedars.
Here, plastic and wet metal, asphalt and the trundling forklifts.
And nothing will come of this rain
but money

and part of a truck.

NEIL WATT'S POEM

At first metal does not know what it is.

It has lived so long in the rock
it believes it is rock.
It thinks as a rock thinks: ponderous,
weighty, taking a thousand years to reach
the most elementary of hypotheses, then hundreds more years
to decide what to consider next.

But in an instant the metal is pulled into the light.
Still dizzy with the astounding speed
with which it is suddenly introduced to the open air
it is processed through a concentrator
before it can begin to think how to respond.
Not until it is hurtling along on a conveyor belt
is it able to inquire of those around it
what is happening?
We are ore, is the answer it gets.

A long journey, in the comfortable dark. Then the confusing
noise and flame of the smelter, where the ore
feels nothing itself, but knows it is changing
like a man whose tooth is drilled under a powerful anaesthetic.
Weeks later, the metal emerges as a box full of bolts.
What are we? it asks. *Three-quarter-inch bolts.*

The metal feels proud about this. And that is a feeling
it knows it has learned since it was a stone
which in turn makes it feel a little awed.
But it cannot help admiring its precise hexagonal head,
the perfectly machined grooves of its stem.
Fine-threaded, someone says, reading the side of the box.
The bolt glows, certain now it is destined for some amazing purpose.

Then it comes out of its box and is pushed
first into a collar, *a washer,* and then
through a hole in a thin metal bar.
Another washer is slipped on, and something
is threaded along the bolt, something else
that is made of metal, *a nut,* which is whirled in tight

with great force. The head of the bolt
is pressed against the bar of metal it passes through.
After a minute, it knows the nut around itself
holds a bar of metal on the other side.

Nothing more happens. The bolt sits astonished
grasping its metal bars. It is a week before it learns
in conversation with some others

it is part of a truck.

ROUTINES

After a while the body doesn't want to work.
When the alarm clock rings in the morning
the body refuses to get up. "You go to work if you're so keen,"
it says. "Me, I'm going back to sleep."
I have to nudge it in the ribs to get it out of bed.
If I had my way I'd just leave you here, I tell it
as it stands blinking. *But I need you to carry your end of the load.*
I take the body into the bathroom
intending to start the day as usual with a healthy dump.
But the body refuses to perform.
Come on, come on, I say between my teeth.
Produce, damn you. It's getting late.
"Listen, this is all your idea," the body says.
"If you want some turds so badly you provide 'em.
I'd just as soon be back in bed."
I give up, flush, wash, and go make breakfast.
Pretty soon I'm at work. All goes smoothly enough
until the first break. I open my lunchpail
and start to munch on some cookies and milk.
"Cut that out," the body says, burping loudly.
"It's only a couple of hours since breakfast.
And two hours from this will be lunch, and two hours after that
will be the afternoon break. I'm not a machine
you can force-feed every two hours.
And it was the same yesterday, too...."
I hurriedly stuff an apple in its mouth to shut it up.

By four o'clock the body is tired
and even more surly. It will hardly speak to me
as I drive home. I bathe it, let it lounge around.
After supper it regains some of its good spirits.
But as soon as I get ready for bed it starts to make trouble.
Look, I tell it, *I've explained this over and over.*
I know it's only ten o'clock but we have to be up in eight hours.
If you don't get enough rest, you'll be dragging around all day
tomorrow again, cranky and irritable.
"I don't care," the body says. "It's too early.
When do I get to have any fun? If you want to sleep
go right ahead. I'm going to lie here wide awake
until I feel good and ready to pass out."

18

It is hours before I manage to convince it to fall asleep.
And only a few hours after that the alarm clock sounds again.
"Must be for you," the body murmurs. "You answer it."
The body rolls over. Furious, and without saying a word,
I grab one of its feet and begin to yank it toward the edge of the bed.

THE DEATH OF THE FAMILY

"You married, Tom?"
>   *No, but the girl I'm going with is.*
> *To someone else. Ha-ha. You see....*

But they aren't listening.

>   "Tom, I was going with a woman
for two years. A few weeks ago she asked if I was going to marry her.
I told her I might someday, but, hell,
I was married all those years
and once I got my divorce I'm not in any hurry to do it again.
I didn't say I wouldn't *ever* marry her.
I just said I didn't want to right now.

"She says to me: 'Dave, if you don't want to marry me
I'm wasting my time.' And that was it.
I tried to call her up a couple of times
but she said if I didn't hang up she would hang up on me.
Bang. Just like that she stopped seeing me.
I think she's crazy. I know she hasn't been seeing anyone else
but she'd rather sit at home and see nobody
than go around with me anymore if I won't marry her.
I just want someone to visit after work, to go dancing with.
And there's something else: she once told me
if we got married, she would come first.
She meant, before my kids. I have two, and there's her three
but she says she has to come first.
There's no way: my kids come first with me.
Who else is there to look after them?"

>   And young Bob
over from Cab Build for the morning, to help out when we're behind:

"My Mom walked out on us twice.
After the first time, when she wanted to return
my Dad he took her back and it was okay for a while.
Then she left again. And you should see the guy she went off with:
a drunk and everything."

>   Then through his mouth
the voice of his father: "We treated her like a queen

but it wasn't enough for her."

All over the plant, through the long hours.
Up to Test to replace a grille's side shell, I hear Jim Pope's steady voice:
"When my first wife left me, I phoned in to take the day off.
I had the locks changed by ten o'clock, and was down to the bank
to make sure she didn't get a cent.
Then I went over to check about the car registration.
You have to move fast when it happens...."

Someone in the small group of coveralls
is receiving advice.

BOB KINE'S SONG

I got those
Monday morning blues.
I got those
Monday morning blues.
Right down to the bottom of my steel-toed shoes.

Spent the whole night looking at the alarm clock,
had it set for six-fifteen.
Spent the whole night looking at the alarm clock.
I had it set for six-fifteen.
Woke up at seven-thirty: O Lord, I'm late for work again.

Jumped in my car and drove
as fast as it would go.
Jumped in my car and drove it just as fast as it would go.
Ran out of gas on the freeway; cold rain falling, mixed with snow.

Found a phone booth and called the foreman:
told him what my troubles were this time.
Yes, I phoned in to tell the foreman what my troubles were this time.
He said: "Bob, you were late three times last week, missed eleven days
in the past two months and left early eight times since January...."
—I should have saved my dime.

And when I got to the factory
he had me back on the rivet crew.
Yes, when I finally got to the factory he put me back on the rivet crew.
Bucking those rivets all day with Schultz: don't know if I can make it
    through.

So I went upstairs to the washroom
to snort some coke and take my ease.
Went upstairs to the washroom to snort some coke and take my ease.
Just when I have it unwrapped on the paper, then of course I had to
    sneeze.

And I forgot my lunch money:
eating a candy-bar one more time.

Yes, I forgot my lunch money: eating a candy-bar one more time.
If I don't get out of this factory, people, I'm about to go out of my
    mind.

I got those
Monday morning blues.
I got those Monday morning blues.
Lordy, Lordy, right down to the bottom of my
steel-
      toed
         shoes.

VIOLENCE

The cars leap out of the plant parking lot
lay rubber, fishtail, and disappear.

Bill says: "The scar? When I was up in Ashcroft
I was coming out of the pub one day and a guy I'd never seen
smacked me in the face with a piece of wood.
Broke these teeth and split me open along here: nose, lips, chin.
I got stitched up, and the next day
had a buddy drive me around town looking for the guy.
I saw him, told my buddy to stop
and leaped out holding a tire iron behind my back.

"The guy recognized me. He comes up and says:
'I'm sure sorry about yesterday. I thought you were somebody else.'
I said to him: 'You have three seconds to start running.'
He turned to get away, and I let him have it across the back of the head.
Cold-cocked him right there in the street.
Then I kicked the shit out of him, broke a couple of his ribs
and me and my buddy got out of there fast."

And Magnowski, the giant partsman, on his wedding night:
"They put shaving cream, lather, all over my car.
I stopped in at a garage to wash it off
and as I was using the hose the attendant comes out
and just stands there, making all these dumb comments
like: 'I guess you're really gonna screw her tonight, boy.'
I couldn't believe it. He was big, but
I'm a head taller than him. I was going to deck him
but it was our wedding night. Debbie was right there in the car
and I'm wearing a tuxedo and everything.
So I just said: 'Do you have a hose with some *pressure*
in it, asshole?' He got kind of choked up at that.
He could see I was really mad, just holding myself in.

"But I didn't want to ruin it for Debbie on our wedding.
I think I'm going back this Saturday and see if the guy is still on."

And Don Grayson, another partsman, limping around
with a broken foot he got kicking someone

in a fight in the Duff beer parlor.
He and his friends took exception to some remarks
that were made about the woman who brings the food.
And me always careful not to get in a fight.
Chris and Ernie, Bucket and Phil at lunch one day
talking about a brawl, and me saying:
"It takes two to fight. If you don't want to
you can always walk away." And Ernie really horrified
at this: "Oh no, Tom, no, no.
There are times when you have to fight, you just have to."
And me maintaining that you don't
and everybody looking disgusted at my idea.

How is it I have clung all my life to my life
as though to the one thing I never wanted to lose?

Bob changes the subject. We begin to talk about car accidents.

INDUSTRIAL MUSIC

for Michael Millar, Michael Taylor, Gary Walsh

After a hundred years they paused
and they heard
music; other things were on the wind
but they heard a music filling in the continent behind them:
their own music, which grew slowly,
starting at the quietest moments
like a flower, or at prayer, and at
work, and then beginning to be pumped through
cash registers, radios, and finally even leaked in
through small grilles in elevators.

But as fast as the melodies get smoothed
into a dollar, a man stands up in a noisy bar and
begins to sing, and another man joins him and
another, until the air is filled again with music,
human voices. And twenty thousand of us
are put in a single vast room
to hear one famous voice with a song rise through amplifiers
and the songs also come from just Bob Garrison
driving his '55 Willys up the Canyon from Siska
on a rainy Saturday and only me and one other
jammed into his front seat listen.

And I remember in the truck factory Boris Hukaluk drumming
everywhere, standing in Cab Electrical
tapping out the intricate rhythms with his wire stripper
and a screwdriver, but Boris also
knows everything about Folding Hoods after years
working at that before, so he gets assigned back on the days
Hoskins doesn't show. And I asked him there
why he didn't ever become a professional musician and he said
I didn't like the life; too many late nights all the time
so he drums weekends in a cabaret, in the house band
without even a name, and does special jobs at New Year's and
drums through his days and years at the factory
his fingers and pencils falling on the metal. One day
we are up at Test fitting a hood and one of the mechanics
picks up Boris' rhythm and sends it back to him

26

with his wrenches, as best he can, and Boris
grins and stops what he's doing and gives out
another short riff, and this time
a couple of guys try to match him, and Boris laughs
and taps out another complicated run
and this time maybe half a dozen guys start
clumsily pounding away after his lead. And this makes so much noise
(since somebody is banging on a waste can) that the foreman
comes out of his office to find out what's up
but sees Boris and shakes his head and goes back.

Then it's lunch and someone turns a truck radio on, and the music,
rock now, pours into the echoing Test bays
like the wind when somebody rolls aside one of the huge doors
on a cold wet February morning, the wind
flowing in off the river among the parked tires and motors,
the tool boxes, air hoses and containers of oil,
a wind that carries with it all the sounds of the City at work
this day: grudgingly, but alive, and moving.

THE KENWORTH FAREWELL

Everyone wore eyeglasses for safety.
To Wayman at first the factory had the look
of a studious crew of graduate students
dressed by mistake in torn and baggy coveralls
who had wandered in through the high aisles of stacked parts
to stand aimlessly amid the machines and assembly stations.

And the boys in Cab Build
were hooting: *Whoop. Whoop.*

Settling in, getting to know the place, Wayman discovered
both box-end and open-end wrenches, fine- and coarse-threaded nuts.
Also the forklifts, which never failed to release
a warm fart of propane when Wayman passed behind them.
And Wayman meanwhile got real intimate with his wristwatch:
staring at each minute in every hour
until somehow it turned into a morning, and even an entire day.

And the boys in Cab Build
were hooting: *Whoop. Whoop.*

Wayman returned home each late afternoon to the rebirth of a bath:
the grand feel of fresh clothes against his skin.
Picking the dirt out of his nose, he understood
not only was he in the factory, the factory was in him, too.

So he learned all the Kenworth slogans:
"It's only a truck," and "It's only a Kenworth,"
and "At sixty miles an hour, who is going to know the difference?"
Also: "There's a right way, a wrong way,
and a Kenworth way." And Wayman mastered
the Great Kenworth Fault Game: "It isn't *my* fault."
Even if an error took only a minute to fix
like forgetting to drill safety light holes, for example,
everyone argued happily for hours
all the cosmic questions and implications
of each other's ultimate innocence and guilt.

Wayman learned the faces, and what each meant.
Working with young Bill was a rain of washers

he and Larry endlessly tossed back and forth.
Wayman discussed women with so many, only to later discover
they were just out of high school and still living at home.
And there was the day Gerry the foreman complained about the quota:
"I have seven hoods to get out today, but what do I have
to do it with? A hunky (meaning Daniluk)
a hippie (meaning Wayman)
and a God damn sky pilot...."(meaning Wayne
who before Wayman left finally cornered him
and gave him one pamphlet on the Four Spiritual Laws
and another called—Wayne said: "Don't worry about the title"—
Jesus and the Intellectual.)

And the boys in Cab Build
were hooting: *Whoop. Whoop.*

Wayman might have stayed forever.
But his first clue was a Monday morning
when it seemed the weekend had never occurred.
The second clue was Paul Palmer telling him
(Palmer the mainstay of the Pipe Shop's
Hose Amputation Division):
"I've worked at this bench a year, but it feels as though
I might have been here one day, or always."
And so often the great gleaming $50,000 trucks
wouldn't start at the end of the Final Line
and had to be towed out into the yard—which broke Wayman's heart.
Also there was a moment when Wayman found himself
in his own car rolling down the highway near Bellingham:
heading north again on a Sunday, but driving just the same
on that beautiful concrete freeway which he knows also drifts
south in a dream towards California.

So Wayman at the end picked up his toolbox
shook hands with the foreman
and walked out another time through the Kenworth Keyhole:
that man-sized door set into a truck-sized door
on which someone has thoughtfully painted "Door."
Wayman passed out of the world of tires and fiberglass dust,

timeclocks, and the long sessions upstairs in the can.

And as the boys in Cab Build
howled their last farewell: Wayman
was on his way once more.

TOOL FONDLE

After some months, I take out my toolbox
and open it. Under the lid
is the tray, jammed with so many metal shapes
nestled together: my box-end wrenches of various sizes,
my ratchet and the necessary sockets
plus an extension bar, and one deep 7/16ths socket,
a cold chisel, a drift, a center punch, pliers,
and a device Bill MacKay made for me: a Phillips head
from a power screwdriver mounted into a small angled brace,
useful for attaching a hood stop cable to its mount on an engine block.

These are of dull or silvery metal. Then there are colors:
the yellow plastic handles of my assorted screwdrivers,
the deep luminous blue of the 3/8ths nutdriver handle.
A dirty cream case for my Lufkin measuring tape. An orange
cardboard package of Swedish ear cotton.
And tucked into the socket section of the tray:
some white Band-Aids, a few sticks of spearmint gum,
a pencil, red-and-white union button
and a black felt marker pen.

Slipped between the tray and the back of the toolbox
is a blank perforated time card
and above that, taped to the inside of the box lid,
are notes to myself: how to attach wear plates,
the dimensions of the aircleaner cutout
on a 736 metal hood blank (wrong, according to Jim Pope)
and finally some numbers to account for time spent
at unitglass trim, fender trim (for the hours
we were sent up to Cab Trim when they were behind)
and also the clean-up number which is useful every day.

Then, lifting out the heavy tray, underneath
in the bottom of the box are my gloves, a hacksaw,
a wire stripper, right- and left-hand metal shears (new)
and an old coil of twine handy for tying back a fiberglass hood
on a truck, to keep the grille from resting on the bumper
if you have to stand inside and it's short a stop cable.
Also my wooden-handled hefty ball-peen

31

hammer, with the wood taped where it joins the head
just in case. And one of the little yellow cardboard hood tags
useful for writing things down on.

And with all these, I built more than a thousand trucks.
Eight trucks a day for eight months:
not me alone, of course, but pulling these out
and putting them away each day
and sometimes lugging the whole heavy lot
here and there in the plant (along with about
four hundred other people similarly wandering around
and working) more than a thousand trucks at the end of Final Line
got started up, belching black smoke, or else didn't do anything
and had to be towed out into the yard
but at least were assembled.

And my grey metal toolbox used to sit every day
on a shelf next to Andy's, which was larger
as is only fitting, since he was there ten years before me
having built maybe twelve thousand trucks (allowing for the years
when lots less than eight were made each day.) And my box
was larger than Ernie's, who hardly had any tools
and was there only five months before he left,
borrowing from my box as he wanted something
the way I borrowed from Andy's at the start
and even later, if there was something Andy had that I needed
—a small bucking block, for example.

But one day, like Ernie, I closed my lid as usual
and then picked the box up (surprised once more
at the weight of all that metal)
and left for good, leaving Andy's box
still there, ready to be opened again Monday
morning, to go on building trucks
while mine
came home to a closet, where it sits
in the dark—except when I open it
for a few domestic repairs, or when a friend
wants to borrow a certain tool to work on a car.

And across the room from the closet

I've gone back to writing things down
on a typewriter, for a while
(and lots less than eight a day, too).
But every so often I get out my tools
for no good reason and stare at them.

I always meant to get a good vicegrip
and a file. Maybe I'll go downtown tomorrow
and see what they're asking.

FOR THE SERGEANT, GONE TO JESUS

Ulcers bleed, not only in the fat rich.

There are young men who also puke blood
black blood, gagging and retching

Who come to sit in Emergency and look at the wall.
They notice the corridor's baseboards
the kind of job done by the wallboard tapers.

Here is one who knows the Jews did it to him.
They paid him two-fifty an hour for cutting scrap.
No union, his hands and legs burned by the hot metal.

He fell almost a floor working demolition.

The government did it to him.
They told his parents to sell their cattle and grow wheat.
When the money was all in machinery, they said *buy animals again.*

The corporations did it.
Laying track into a mineshaft up North
the crew was all immigrants but him, driving him back to the city.
At a meeting a man told him: *smash capitalism.*
Everything will be all right then.

Women did it.
He drove across three provinces
to get married. In debt for the car.
In debt for the ring. Sandy always able to work:
insurance company secretary.
Forty dollars for forty hours, take-home.
Nothing to do after work but drive around visiting friends.

Beer did it. What do you do, unemployed?
Nothing to do. Lie around the house like a woman:
sweep up a little, nothing to read,
nothing to figure out, nothing to carry or lift.
Wait for the mailman. Wait for pogey. Wait
for a job-letter. Wait for a phone call.

Wait for another round, down at The Anchor.

The police did it. And they did it without ever writing his name.
Do you want to know about crime? About breaking the law?
All you have to do is have no money.
Nothing to wait for that is going to come.
No prospects. Then
you will understand everything.
The law will become so clear to you it will disappear.
Should it ever return it will be in the form of money.

Or Jesus. Sweet Jesus. Clearer than acid, cleaner than weed.
Who explains. Yes, He does. *The Spirit*
tells me what to do.
You know that Jesus loves you?

And the rest of us, his friends, are sailors
manning the houses ranked along our streets:
houses that steam on relentlessly through the weather
and the holy, ulcerous nights.

THE UNEMPLOYMENT INSURANCE COMMISSION
POEMS: 2. A CURSING POEM

This poem curses the Unemployment Insurance Commission.
This poem curses it.
This poem curses it in the center
and on the left hand and on the right.
It curses each clerk and official
every benefit control officer
who does not flare up like a fire in the night
and cry down the masters of the Commission
and drag them out, the mad animals who have turned them
into the policemen of lives.
Let them tear off their own shirts
and cry in the streets for pity
for the nation they have built
out of anger and black despair.
Where do they think a man goes
when they turn him away?
Where does a woman go
on two-thirds of a salary already not enough?
They turn into a country of hatred and fear.

Then let them cry this out.
Let them cry for forgiveness
for it is they who have fashioned a nation of clear wind
into a pit of tar.
Let them leave quickly now
so the wickets stand empty, the tills ajar
no one standing behind the counters.
Let them move to the rear of the line-ups facing themselves.
Otherwise the curse of this poem will strike them.

A small red maple leaf
will appear in both of their eyes.
Everyone will see that they are *Canadian*.
Each one knows what a *Canadian*
does to his countrymen.

That is the curse of the center.
And Welfare is on the left hand, where you go

when there is no money.
This poem curses it.
That one person should hand another so tiny a sum
and ask him to live out his days on it
in this country
cannot be forgiven.

Though they pretend this woman will drink away the money
they cannot be forgiven for what they do to a single life.
Though they complain that this one is retarded
they cannot be forgiven
for what they do to a single life.
Though they say this one could get a job
if he really wanted to
no one sees them leaving their own odious work
to get the other job they could find if they really wanted to.
They believe that the poor are the same as themselves
but have fallen from grace. For this
there is no forgiveness.
I cannot forgive them. Jesus cannot forgive them.
In the eyes of every man and woman they meet
is their curse: they will burn with shame
through their lives on the ground.

And on the right hand is Manpower.
Manpower is a slime, it is a room of fools.
They exist to dispense jobs that do not exist.
They are a palace of lies: upgrading courses
that do not lead anywhere; faked statistics
based upon work paying less than a loaf
promoted by men who have already stuffed themselves this day.

This poem curses it.
It names it a mouth, of useless advice:
"The yellow pages are full of jobs. Begin with the A's."
But it is a mouth with teeth, the teeth of rats:
"If you do not co-operate with us
your unemployment benefits will be withdrawn."
So it is a sink of oil
all the arrogance of those with jobs
talking to those without:

"Do you know how to conduct yourself at an interview?"
This poem curses it, stupidity grown so fine
it appears as thin as paper.
It is the curse on everyone who lies:
none of them shall escape. They will dig a hole
in the weary sand. Presently they will be told
to fill it in. Soon
they will be directed to dig it out once more.

THE COUNTRY OF EVERYDAY: WORKPLACE

The defeat of any jobshop: dusty windows
and a long scrape down the cement of one wall.
These will not be restored unless the company collapses
or moves, and the new owner decides to paint.
Each day, now, the same smudged interior.

This is the inside of a building no one will ever love.
It is like a mine shaft thousands of feet under the earth:
a place we only descend into for labor.
The broom misses the corners. Dirt
grows on the tops of the baseboard heaters.

The place fills with the sadness of anything
herded together, with a weariness
like the sound of the noon hooter
or the foreman's whistle, pushing us back on the site after lunch.
The room is tired of being kept awake all night.
One shift is the same as another.
Even if the fluorescent lamps are shut down
this room in the darkness holds only work.
That is all it has known: nothing else
will ever be brought out of this mine.

Even the demolition crews will be sweating
as their crowbars start to pull the wiring from the walls.

THE COUNTRY OF EVERYDAY: 12

About the second day, the foreman told us
he wanted one corner of the site cleared.
So we started moving a huge pile of beams
blackened with dirt, that had been ripped down
when the building's interior was gutted.
Mark and I worked almost two hours
carrying the beams across the width of the site.

There is a terrible fatigue that begins in the body.
This is not the abrupt refusal of legs
that are new at the job to keep unloading lumber.
Nor when hands still soft suddenly uncurl
from around a board that can no longer be lifted.
This is a heaviness like a deep grief,
a weariness that slowly works up from under the earth
passing through the soles of the boots into all the body.
This is Newson at the end of his shift
too tired to take off his plywood mill shoes:
falling asleep dressed on the bed, or in a chair
or with one boot off, the heavy leather of the other
dropping out of his hand onto the floor.

The beams were rough-edged, splintered. The foreman
had us move them back across the site a week later, when he wanted
the further corner. This time we stacked them properly:
a row of them, then two-by-fours crossways, then another row.

And out of the continual weight of the work, a stone
presses inside the body. It is like a piston
rising in the great cylinder of the rib-cage
squeezing the breath, so you gasp and strain for more air.
But when the air already in is compressed enough
a spark ignites, and a tiny flame
begins to burn in the brain like the pilot light of a stove.

This is the flame of hate, of the madness of labor.
This is why there is such rage when our checks are delayed.
Why we crash the metal scaffolding down as we disassemble it
like a garbageman tossing empty cans back onto the driveway.
This is why some of us retreat into doing very intricate work:

skilled finishing lace-like carpentry,
a hand cupped carefully around the flame so that no one will see.

Mark and I moved the thick beams a day after that.
The foreman wanted the first corner again, so we piled them outside
at the rear in the lane.

But the light always burns. It waits
for a new gust of fuel so it can roar into fire.
That is why one shrieks with the nail that bends as he drives it.
Why even the foreman tosses his hammer through a pane of glass
when the owner leaves the site after his daily tour.
That is why there is so much drunk.
But the flame singes the edge of the beer, and sometimes
the fluid ignites: fire burns along the surface,
black smoke pouring into the brain. Fists
fly into faces, connect, the tables turn and the cheap glasses
smash into chips and foam. The bouncers move into the center of it
and then the door looms up, and outside
are all the indifferent faces of the street.

After the rains began, Mark and I brought the soaked beams inside;
the foreman said he didn't want them to get any wetter.

Always the low flame. When it has burned long enough
the cavity where it flickers in the mind hardens.
Without saying a word, without a single electrical nerve
passing from the back of the brain down to the belly
every part of the body knows it is scum.

The knowledge is a wind that shakes the body, a wind
blowing continually like breath
brings the fire of oxygen to the furnaces of the cells.
You are scum. An object
owned by the company
like a crummy or a shovel. You are worse than that:
you are replaceable. You are not so necessary to the project
as paint. That is what the body knows.

And when the job ended, the owner thought
it would be useful to salvage the beams. Mark and I
spent an afternoon hauling them outside again

and carrying them down the lane to the other building.
We stacked each beam inside there.

This is the madness: a young man crouched over like a child
his head between his knees, only breathing. The body
at last treated by you as any chalk-line or broom
so even off the job the body is driven like a car
whose payments you can't meet: use it,
get your money's worth, run the fucking thing
before it is repossessed once more and taken away.

THE COUNTRY OF EVERYDAY: THE DANCER

She returns at the end of the party
to the room where the dancing was; a few guests
sprawl in the armchairs, as though stunned
by the rock still pounding from the stereo.

She returns alone. Under the exhausted stares
of the watchers, in the dim light, she begins to dance.

And reaches for the music with her body.
Beneath sweatshirt and jeans, her beautiful heavy breasts
her lovely full hips and flanks, slowly ease her toward the sound.

Till she finds it. As the music enters her
she tries to clutch it, to hold it in against
her knees and thighs, her coaxing belly and breasts.
Her body is gripped in the beat and shudder.

She is dancing her job: working out
days making locks, the three parts
to the work of her department.
Loading in tumblers, two days a week
five to a lock-blank, according to the number
stamped on a newly cut key. Her hands
getting raw and thick from the work
dipping into the bins of tumblers
and the tray-load of fresh blanks.
Then two days inserting pins and springs
into the blanks, the company having decided
task rotation keeps down boredom to increase production.
Then two days checking the loaded locks.
But every evening, making her lunch on the kitchen table
she faces eight hours again, two cigarette breaks
and eating at noon at the same table
with the girls of her section, their chatter
of good times and boyfriends.

Before this she worked in a place that made cosmetics.

And here, on a Friday night, she dances
the dream of the girls from the plant: that they will not do this

all their lives. She dances the feverish whispers
the low, breaking voices in the bed, the marriage
that frees them from timeclock and coathook and the bus each day.
But she also knows that the new husband's face
room after room, begins to fill the entire apartment
like the smell of gas. So she dances the color of sinks
how to vacuum a floor, and at last re-applying for her old job
as a foodstore cashier. Stepping alone in her serious beauty
she follows as well a different dream:
of a red time, pamphlets and meetings
speeches, and what is going to happen.
We won't make locks, she says. *No one will need them then.*

Now she sways to a hard music
in a room almost dark. Her nipples move
against the cloth of her shirt, sweat forms in the groin
as she flows with the sound. Her eyes are shut
as if she dances asleep
in a room of sleepers. And no one knows
the dream to awaken her.

THE COUNTRY OF EVERYDAY: DEATH, DEATH

Why is there so much here about death? Because the face is a mask
behind which is a jar of fluid and water:
a bottle of muck. When the bones of the face
are pushed in, the skull is forced out at the back.
A substance pours out of the flesh
and spreads in wet lumps over the ground.

Sometimes the chin is still recognizable, as in
a photograph of a logging truck accident.
Sometimes you can tell which part was the forehead
as when a drill bangs back, catching the operator
under what were his eyes.

There is so much of death, because Rae says
on the Portage Mountain Dam they were told
the company budgeted for one hundred and twenty men to die
during construction. And not a single executive
was expected to perish from ulcers or heart attack
during the whole of the project.

And when the monthly totals, Rae said
fell far below the projected figures
the foremen began cutting the weekly safety meetings
and advising crew chiefs to do the same.
And one of Rae's friends was killed at the damsite.
And as they had all made a pact to get drunk
if any of them did die
they all went out and got stinking together
and it only took Rae seven beers.

There is so much of death, because
there is a demolition man who was caught
as a house wall broke in, when they had shored it up
with the cheap two-by-fours provided by the company.
And he jumped out a window, and his friend
working inside with him didn't and was crushed.

And he said: "The stupid son-of-a-bitch waited too long
deciding what to do. It was his own fault."

Death, death because there is a war on, and
one side is losing.

THE COUNTRY OF EVERYDAY:
LITERARY CRITICISM

"He was in a hurry," Wood said, "the young foreman
only 26, down on his knees at the base of
the heavy lamppost, impatient to push it back on the block.
He was yelling at the rest of us to give him a hand
and didn't see the top of the pole, as it
swayed over and touched the powerline.

"I was looking right at him. There was a flash
and he just folded over onto his side and
turned black: his ears melted.
There were two holes burned in the pavement
where his knees were. Somebody started giving him
mouth-to-mouth, and I said *forget it. I mean, he's dead."*

And there are poets who can enter in
to the heart of a door, and discover the rat inside us
that must be kept caged in the head because it is perfectly sane.

There are poets who claim to know what it's like
to have a crucifix wedged in the throat
unable to swallow, and how the knot of the stomach
turns into a bowl of fire.

But around and ahead of them
is the housewife endlessly washing
linoleum, sheets, fruit dishes, her hands
and the face of a child. And there is the girl who stands
in the cannery line twelve hours in season
to cut out the tips of the fish.
For the paper they tear out to write on
is pulled from the weeks of working graveyard
and all the weariness of millwork, the fatigue
of keeping it going, the urge to reclaim the body
for the hours not working or sleeping
when the body ends too tired for much but a beer and a laugh.

Beside every dazzling image, each line
desperate to search the unconscious
are the thousand hours someone is spending

watching ordinary television.
For every poet who considers the rhythm
of the word "dark" and the word "darkness"
a crew is balancing high on the grid
of a new warehouse roof, gingerly taking the first load of lumber
hauled thirty feet up to them.

For every hour someone reads critical articles
Swede is drunk in a bar again
describing how he caught his sleeve once in the winch of an oil rig
whirling him round till his ribs broke.
And for every rejection of a manuscript
a young apprentice is riding up on the crane
to work his first day on high steel.
"Left my fingerprints in the metal
when I had to grab a beam to get off," he says.
And Ed Shaw stands looking down into the hold
where a cable sprang loose lifting a pallet
and lashed across the dock, just touching one of the crew
whose body they are starting to bring up from the water.

When the poet goes out for a walk in the dusk
listening to his feet on the concrete, pondering
all of the adjectives for rain, he is walking on work
of another kind, and on lives that wear down like cement.
Somewhere a man is saying, "Worked twenty years for the City
but I'm retired now."
Sitting alone in a room, in the poorhouse of a pension
he has never read a modern poem.

CUMBERLAND GRAVEYARD, FEBRUARY 1973

I stand with one hand on the wet uneven rock
that marks the grave of Ginger Goodwin
at Cumberland cemetery in the drizzle of
a Wednesday afternoon: a meadow hacked out of the rainforest
littered with old and new stone markers,
grey cement slabs, and the damp mounds of fresh earth.

In the rain, Cumberland graveyard
looks like the one on Kaien Island where I grew up
in the shadow of Mount Hays, where people said
I'd hate to be buried there and have rainwater
trickling down my back forever.

But they got buried anyway. And here
there are not so many graves as I thought
considering the long chain of coalmine disasters
that ran south from here seventy miles, for nearly
one hundred years. There are few markers that say
Killed in an Explosion in No. 4 Mine; Aged 17 years.
When people get around to putting up stones
they don't seem to care how death arrives, but carve:
Only Sleeping; Lo, I am with you always; and *Gone Home.*
Lots of the graves are neglected now—not as abandoned
as the Chinese cemetery half a mile up the road—
but inscriptions have worn away, headstones tilted
and cracked, and here a slab of old pebbly concrete
above some graves shakes as you walk on it. A few of these slabs
have sagged and split open. You can crouch
and peer in, but inside is only the top of more wet earth
and a few broken plastic flowers
blown across and down from the more modern graves.

A strange familiarity appears in the plots marked
Gran, or *Papa, Mama* and *Mary,* or
In loving memory of our son Tommy, when now
no one can make out the surname. And where the graves
are clear as the Hudson family's, say
—infants, children, parents and the last date in the 1950s—
what would bring anyone out in this rain

to stand looking at the letters chiselled into the blocks of soaking stone?

But Goodwin's grave differs from these.
Not that it's by itself, on the contrary
you could just about get another one beside him
but the rest of the way around he's completely hemmed in
and there's a new pile of wet earth not ten feet away.
Yet Goodwin seems buried
for another reason than these: nobody bothered to put
his birthdate on his stone, for example,
just that he was *Shot, July 26th, 1918.*
And the lettering isn't nearly as regular
as on the other stones: *Lest We Forget* it says
and it's about as professional as a title
someone has put on a pamphlet they've printed
overnight, trying their best with the letters
but not doing so well, and the whole thing soon forgotten
anyway. On the top of the stone
is a crude sickle and hammer—done
as though in the years before there were Commies,
when those who thought a certain way were sure
that what had just happened in Russia
had something in it for them. Like the words
it's an amateur's job: the sort of sickle and hammer
someone might carve if he'd only heard about it
or seen it drawn by hand on a piece of paper. Under it all
in place of a slogan, it says *A Worker's Friend*
like a dog is man's best friend, except that the worn cement curb
that outlines the grave is exactly the size
of a man, not so small as a child or as large as a family.

The afternoon I was there, the grooves in the rock
that form the words were painted black, with fresh red color
for the verb "shot" and the symbol above.
And that's the secret to this wet grave, this poem
and the dripping old coal town: somebody there
drops by once in a while to see how this rock
bears up under the weather. Maybe only one old man,
an ex-miner who lives on in this valley
where the trees have covered the slag heaps and fills
but are going themselves higher up, missing

in vast swathes cut across the mountains. One old man
in the rain and maybe nobody knows exactly who
and won't until he dies also and then two graves
will decay together, or maybe only one
because who puts up stones for old miners now
when the last mine closed twenty years ago
and no one can say when the old man last worked anyhow?

But right now that oldtimer
is keeping a dream going.
Strange to think of a town like Cumberland
having a dream, after all the lives squeezed from it
—in just a second underground
or in unendurable years and days and hours
aboveground and down, all the grinding horror
of living a Company life for a Company lifetime.
But we know it was Cumberland's dream
at least for a day, because everyone says at that time
a mile of the town appeared to bury Goodwin:
a mile of miners and women and kids
which is a lot of people to bury anybody
especially if they aren't being paid to do it.

Strange to think of a town like Cumberland
not only having a dream, but a hero:
an honest-to-something hero (I don't see
how I can call him less
since he came out of nowhere particular
that anyone knows, and worked in the mines
and struck in the strikes of '13
when the great Canadian militia
terrorized the coalfields for a year, before going off
to die like pigs in the muddy barnyard of France.
And Goodwin meanwhile
didn't kill anybody,
kept working away for a better life
up at Trail, became secretary of the miners there
fighting conscription while he could
and when Blaylock and Cominco wanted him dead
or out of there at least, he went—
though on his own terms—hiding out here

51

until he was shot in the back for it.)

And Goodwin didn't kill anyone
to be a hero, not even a scab or a German
or an Indian, as far as we know, but he thought
and read and he wrote, and he talked to people
—we know all that—and he went to lots of meetings
and probably called too many of them himself.
But because he could do all these things, he was a little different
than the man beside him, but he was anyway, really
—that being the way things are—though this difference
plus having a sort of dream
landed him flat on his back under this rainy meadow
a little earlier than his consumption likely would have gotten him here.

And that's all. I walk out of the graveyard gate
as he can't do any more, and cross the wet asphalt
to the car. He's behind us now, like being wakened in the night
and having the dream you were in hesitate in your mind for a second
then slip down through a hole in the net of the night
and vanish into the solid dark wall of black air.
That dream is lost, what it was forgotten
unless, even years later,
you start another dream in which suddenly you are aware
this is a dream you began once before.

THE CHILEAN ELEGIES:
5. THE INTERIOR

The smell of potatoes just taken out of the earth.
The problem every carpenter faces, where the wood
nearly fits. The man who secretly wants to leave his wife
and only his fantasies keep his sexual life alive.

These things no government can alter or solve.

The lineup in the small bank branch on East Twenty-ninth
after work on Friday: old boots and the shapeless trousers,
short windbreakers whose sleeves end in hands that clutch
the paper that means life. Other lines
that have worried their way into the faces above the eyes.

These mean an ache for money that lasts an entire lifetime
from busfare each morning through to the tiny pension.
These mean it is luck that rules: the wisps of lotteries, horses,
or entering the pool each payday for the best poker hand
that can be gathered from the company's number on your check.

Also, applying when they're hiring: no government
has been able to touch that.

The small towns of the Interior. The railroad towns deep in the forest.
What has the government to do with them?
The struggles of the young teacher
who has arrived to work in the school
mainly of Indians. All the arguing
with the principal, and with the old librarian,
the enthusiasm carried into the desperate classroom.
And the Indians themselves. Their new hall
they built themselves at Lytton, which had to be boarded up
after a month because of the damage. The summer camp
they built twenty miles away in the mountains
where a young boy drowned the second week it was open.
It too is abandoned again to the silence.
Potato chips and Coke the staple food of so many.
And television, television, television....

On the Thompson River, or in Parral

the government is not the government of the Indians,
not of the young teacher, not of the townspeople,
not of the lover, the carpenter, the man who digs potatoes in his yard.

But where a government takes the remotest of steps
to return home to the ground, and when even this small gesture
is embargoed, denounced, plotted against
and at last some incredibly expensive aviation gasoline
is pumped into certain jet fighters donated by another government
existing thousands of miles away
there is a loss that goes deeper than the blood,
deeper than the bodies put into the ground,
that descends to the roots of the mountains
and travels that far down in the crust of the planet
along the continental chains
until all over the world another sorrow is confirmed
in the lives of the poor. Once again
we are made less. There are men and women
who in the cells of the fibers of their being
do not believe the Indians are dying fast enough
do not believe the poor are dying fast enough
do not believe that sickness and hunger,
automobile crashes, industrial disasters
and the daily suicides of alcohol and despair
are ridding the earth of us with sufficient speed.
So they call for the only institution
maintained at the highest possible level of efficiency:
the men with guns and capbadges, willing or conscripted,
whole armies and the tireless police. These are the men
who have made of this planet throughout my life
a vast geography of blood.

*So many shot for subversion in Temuco. So many arrested
for drunkenness in Lytton.*

And there is not a government in the world that wants to abolish
the factory.

WHERE I COME FROM

THE BLUE HOUR

The blue hour begins
on the North Shore mountains
flows down to the harbor's edge
and into the blue blanket of City.
This evening the air has turned
a deep marine blue, that settles over the roads and houses
street lamps and neon, muting the detail of
telephone poles, trees, and the angle of roofs
so the low hills of blue become the ground swell
to a blue anthem, points of light everywhere across it
the ten thousand notes of a song: chorus of downtown
and West End, then the long verses of Kitsilano,
Marpole, Mount Pleasant, Grandview
and the far reach to Capitol Hill.

The color calms the blue water
stretching west past the flashes of Point Atkinson's light
and threads in again among
the tugs and sawdust barges
headed slowly up the Fraser's still north arm.

In this hour, a bus
which has blazed the name of my City
across half a continent
rolls in at last with its riding lights burning
moving up the Oak Street Bridge through the blue air.

HIGHWAY 16/5 ILLUMINATION

South-east of Edmonton, on the road that leads
to Vermilion, Lloydminster, and the Saskatchewan border
I feel coming into me again like
a song about a man born in the country
the joy of the highway: the long road

that reaches ahead through these wooded rises, the farms
that spread their fields out around themselves
flat to the sun, the odor of hay filling the cabin of the car

mile by mile, border after border, horizon
to horizon. The highway stretches away
in all directions, linking and connecting
across an entire continent

and anywhere I point the front wheels
I can go.

FRIENDS LOGGING

One day I hear them stomp up the stairs,
kick at my door again, and here they are.
Whether because of the winter shut-down, just a few days off,
or because the summertime woods are about to burn
they sit, ask a few questions about my life
and then resume logging: the chainsaws start up, sawdust begins flying,
the air of my room fills with smoke,
the smell of the wet forest, and with the sound
of rigging signals, diesel engines, and the first huge cedar toppling.

"Did you hear the one about the little man
—about so high—who comes into camp and asks for a job as a faller?
'Here's a chainsaw,' they tell him, 'let's see what you can do.'
I don't use a saw, he says, *I use this:*
and he holds up a little-bitty axe.
'You can't do anything with that,' they tell him
and he says: *Show me a tree you want cut.*
They do, and in three quick blows
the tree creaks, leans, and crashes down.
'My God,' somebody says, 'where did you learn to fall like that?'
You know the Sahara desert? the little man asks.
'Sure,' they reply, 'but there aren't any trees there.'
There aren't now, the little man says."

And that's only speaking with me. If two of them
arrive at the same time, I have to leap under my chair
after less than a minute once they begin to talk to each other
as spruce, hemlock and fir
start dropping to the ground one by one
all over my room. If I go out
for even a few minutes—to get some beer
or something—when I get back
I can hardly push the door open
because of the tangle of branches and roots,
machinery, and the litter of stumps and logs
filling my room like a jumbled windfall.

"There's this chokerman, see, and he saves up enough money
for a trip to Europe. He's flying along in the plane

over Italy, when the pilot comes on the PA
and says the plane has engine trouble
and they are going to issue parachutes so everybody can bail out.
The chokerman begins yelling for his luggage,
he wants his suitcase, right now.
The stewardess tries to calm him down
but he keeps demanding his bag, so finally
they get it for him. He opens his suitcase
and pulls out all he has inside:
a frayed, kinked, twisted, horrible-looking cable.
'What use is that?' asks the stewardess.
'The plane is going to crash. You need a parachute.'
Not me, says the chokerman. *This damn cable*
will hang up anywhere."

Even they admit it is sometimes too much.
Everyone talks about the job after work,
but who else but these speak about it night and day?
Steve tells me: "I'm lying asleep, first night back in Vancouver,
when a train goes by and blows its whistle: *hoot,* hoot hoot.
Now that's a logging signal
so I start to dream I'm standing in the wrong place
and this gigantic log is bearing down on me...."

And Mark: "We're sitting in the pub talking
about the number of logs we've yarded that day
and about the most anyone has ever yarded that we've heard of.
One of the guys who drives a caterpillar tractor
meanwhile is trying to squeeze past us to get to the can
but nobody is paying much attention.
Finally he says in a loud voice:
Do you mind moving your cold deck
so I can get my cat through?"

On and on: while the waiter refills the table,
the hills get barer and barer
and my words spill across their paper, into the common air.

NOT GETTING HIRED

"Writing? This is an *English* department.
Frankly I can't see what use a writer could be."
And also: "Only one book? My friend,
we have literally dozens of applications from poets.
Unless you've done more than this, I'm afraid you'll just go in the pile."

As well, there was a Bursar and Dean of Instruction
who became incensed at Wayman's subversive notions:
"That's how you'd mark an English paper? Do you never use
any other criteria besides your own subjective opinions?
Just answer the question, Mr. Wayman: yes or no."
There was one of a selection committee who invited Wayman
to attend a lecture on Marxist Aesthetics that afternoon.
In the silence that followed Wayman's reply, the Head
leaned forward gravely: "All of us in the Department are going
you know. We'd be very interested
in your reasons for not wishing to attend."

Then there was an appointment for nine p.m., after a long day
dragging boards all around a jobsite. "Enthusiasm, man!"
the Dean of Curriculum and Instruction wanted, as he pounded
one arm of his chair. "Think big. This college is going places.
You'll have to step lively if you want to come along with us."
And there was a university Wayman was keen to impress, where
    he spoke
with great speed and skill about his plans, his hopes, his ideas.
Later, Wayman heard the Chairman had thoughtfully fingered
a small white pamphlet after Wayman left.
"And did you notice his pupils?" the Chairman had asked.
"How large they were? Obviously, the man is on drugs."

Everywhere, the impossible gigantic question:
"Now if you were setting up a basic composition program
how would you go about it?" And: "We find in our classes sometimes
we can utilize other media besides print. How do you feel about this?"
One night, a horrible dream
in which Wayman goes to see Neil at the site
to ask for his old job back, and finds Neil has appointed
a selection committee: Danny, Pat Flynn and John Davies

sit waiting amid the scaffolds and sawdust.
Danny asks the first question: "Now, Wayman,
lately we've been putting our gyproc nails
eight inches apart. What are your thoughts on that?"

Everyone's eyes turn toward him, watching.

FRIDAY NIGHT IN EARLY SEPTEMBER AT MORRIS AND SARA WAYMAN'S FARM, ROSENEATH, ONTARIO

At dusk, the grey wooden barn
drops anchor near the house
like a huge ship riding up at the top of the fields.
On the barn roof, against the lighter part of the sky
pigeons flutter and call. Silence everywhere else
except for a car speeding by on the road.

It's an old barn: inside in the day
the wide beams show adze marks
from when they were squared by hand. Age
is what this ship carries
besides the hay hoisted in each year
to the upper decks
and the cattle loaded aboard below late in the fall.
And she has held other cargo: two years ago
her bins were full of oats; the farmer who rents the land
trucked his crop to Peterborough
to find the cereal manufacturers there wouldn't pay enough
to meet his costs. So he drove back in a rage
and dumped the oats here.

It was always a difficult farm: each inch of it
cut out of the forest; stones down in the fields
had to be levered out each spring before plowing.
Now only beef is grown: the farmer runs his herd
on four such farms owned by city people.
This property was bought when an old woman died.
She had lived in fewer and fewer rooms, sealing off
the upstairs, then parts of the main floor,
until her life was the bedroom and an adjoining kitchen.
The present owners use the place summers and weekends.

This evening, in the dim vegetable garden
the corn is finished, the tomatoes and carrots
are ready for picking. Just before dark
the fields look exhausted,
cropped close by the cattle in their daily tidal drift over the land.
The animals are out of sight now, on the slope of the furthest hill.
At dawn they will be up around the barn again

as it floats into the morning
with the first of the chill air it will haul all winter
already stored in its holds.

THINNING CARROTS

On a July afternoon, squatting between the rows
of the farm garden, thinning carrots: for a foot or so ahead
I pull out the thin creepers,
miniature vines that tug out easily,
then the various broad-leaved weeds, a single blade of grass,
and something with a stalk
a quarter of an inch wide
—huge, in this small jungle.

The carrot greens are like tough threads
rising in clumps where too many were planted.
My thick fingers
go in like a clumsy tailor's
to find the healthiest among them and try
to separate that one from the cluster on all sides,
clearing the earth around it.
From each rejected top
dangles a tiny orange carrot.
But the soil is dry, and sometimes
my fingers snag the one I mean to leave.
Or else I'll hook one stem of a two-stemmed plant
so both come free, opening more space than I want.
But then it's too late, and I poke into the next dense stretch

as I move slowly forward,
simplifying each inch of the line.

JEWS

A weird family to come from
like most families. And if you trace it back
you have to stop at the great-grandparents:
the most distant lives anyone remembers.
Behind them, only a few names
can be recalled.

Herschel, born in 1897
my father's mother's brother
remembers *his* father
Louis Altschuler, born 1859
in Russia, lived in Mglin
also known as Amlin.
Louis trained as a rabbi
but decided it was the rich
who ruled the synagogues.
So he gave it up and in 1899
emigrated to Bracebridge
Ontario, where he worked as a pedlar
carrying all the objects he sold door-to-door,
farmhouse-to-farmhouse, laid out and
wrapped in one huge square of cloth
gathered at the four corners and hoisted
onto his back. By 1904
he had saved enough to bring over
his wife and five children, including Herschel,
so he quit peddling as unsuitable
for a family man and worked
at a number of jobs
and moved to Barrie, and then in 1913
to Toronto, by this time with a sixth child.

Herschel remembers the other Jew in Bracebridge:
a man who made a living
by selling the labor of certain immigrants
for whom he translated, arranged jobs,
collected wages and provided bad housing
while taking a large percentage of what they earned.
Eventually one man protested
and roused up the others

66

so the labor broker fired the troublemaker.
But before he left, the broker
slipped money into his pocket
and then had him arrested for theft.
As the court needed a translator
one of Herschel's brothers was asked.
The broker went to Herschel's father
and appealed to him as a fellow Jew
to order his son to falsify the accused's story
during the trial. Herschel's father refused
saying *this*
is a matter of justice.
But later when the laborer was acquitted
and the broker himself charged,
Herschel's father would permit no word
to be translated against him.
After all, he said, he *is* a Jew.

And isn't this the idea of a family?
You don't want any member to cause harm to somebody else
but at the same time you don't want one of us hurt.

On the other side of my life
it was a similar pattern to get to North America.
My mother's mother, Margaret Matusov
was born near Vitebsk about 1870
and eventually married a carpenter.
They left Russia together,
spent six months in Berlin
and arrived in England about 1895
settling in Newcastle
until 1910, when Joseph left for Canada.
His wife and, by now, four children
went to Liverpool to wait
while he earned the passage money,
lost it gambling, and by 1912 had it again
and the whole family arrived in Toronto.

At every stage of these journeys: life
and death. Margaret's sister
a woman whose name no one I talked to recalls
was with the family as it waited in Liverpool

and met and married a man named Bailey, *Uncle Mushka,*
and stayed. Herschel identifies
an old photograph as one of his brothers
dead of T.B. in northern Ontario before the First World War.

So many people have become
just a name on a chart I made
or at most a few anecdotes and odd facts.
An important date in a life
shrinks from being a particular incident
on a certain day in one of the months
—a moment during which someone
was probably even aware of the weather—
to being just a reference to some hazy
approximate year.

And the family is dwindling: couples now mostly have
one or two children
moving apart on the map, and in their lives.

But is it only the words of a priest, or lines
on a form from the State, or the birth of a child
that can make a family? Over the decades
people have also tried religion and class,
race and the tribe. Myself
I think we have come to another kind of family.
Perhaps now it is just ourselves and our friends
—some of whom we like a lot, and others
we see as little as possible of like any unpleasant relative.

One list I have of my friends
includes a nurse, a seaman, a clerk,
a builder, a printer, a logger, a teacher
and so on. But this doesn't explain who they are
any more than if I wrote down their names:
each with its own family
that can also be traced across this continent to where
it leaps backward over an ocean into another world.

I meet so many people, enjoy them,
live with them or around them for years
and then some turn into words on paper

in a letter, or on a chart.

I believe all these people form a family.
And now I've said that
I think it is up to someone else to worry about
which of them are Jews.

WHERE I COME FROM: GRANDFATHER

A dead man. A dead person,
who ran away from the London Jews and joined
the Royal Sussex Regiment, shipping east
in an old three-decker to India, his pay-book
stamped *Church of England*, under his new
English name. The Regiment
taught him grammar and arithmetic
while he garrisoned the North West Frontier,
had the collar of his uniform shot off,
and was promoted to corporal, but one night
an officer returned to camp drunk
without the proper challenge, so every NCO on duty
—including him—got reduced to the ranks.

Back in England, they say he and his brother
stood in Trafalgar Square and tossed
to decide who would go to Canada and who to South Africa.
Thus my grandfather was awarded Toronto
and a job as a machine operator
for Tip Top Tailors, a wife, a family,
a death, and another wife,
a house on Borden Street eleven-and-a-half feet wide
in a street of Jews, with Jews living upstairs.
He also got a strike, in the midst of the Depression
and only went back to his machine during
another war. In 1945 he was chosen
Inner Guard of the Mozirir Sick and Burial Society
—a social and self-help club for ex-Russian Jews
which he was too, if you went back far enough
though locally he was known for his speech and military bearing
as "the Mayor of Borden Street" or "the Englishman."

In his last years, he refused to give up the house
though he was sick a number of times, and though
the street began to fill with south Italians.
A kid from the neighborhood prepared a meal for him most days
in return for a little money. And his room
began to hold all the clutter and dust of the single elderly poor:
faded snapshots and photographs, a calendar, the same few dishes

70

used every day, a television continually muttering
and mumbling to itself, the bed rumpled and half-made.

When he died, few on the street knew him.
He had to be carried into death by
a step-cousin's band of musicians
who had attended the funeral out of courtesy
and stayed to bear the old man to the grave.
They lifted him into a small shed at the edge of the cemetery
and came out and stood around, while shards of porcelain were put
on his ears, eyes, nose and mouth
to show that in the grave nothing is heard,
nothing seen, nothing smelled, nothing tasted
and nothing said. The first handful of sand from the grave
was put into the coffin, to show
earth to the earth.

        And standing at the open gravesite
the young rabbi with the red band in his hat
who never knew any of us in life or death
but managed anyway to make up a little message about my grandfather
which actually could have been about anybody
now led my father in the halting, word-for-word
repetition of the Kaddish.
Then they turned on the machine for lowering the coffin
and flung a mat of synthetic grass
over the slowly descending box, as inside
what was left of what had been my grandfather went down
wrapped in the step-cousin's shawl.

Seven days the candle burned for him: seven days
seven years ago now. And from my grandfather
I got my father, my name,
the ring they took off his body that he had been given
when he made Inner Guard, and I got
a cheap disposable yarmulka handed out from a tray
at the funeral, a skullcap I still have
scrunched up in one pocket of a coat in a closet
kept in case I ever need it again.

CANADA AT WAR

"I'm glad the war's over..." a cheerful voice
"...so no more young men like yourself will be blown to bits."

A faded blue suit and cane had stopped on the sidewalk
and was smiling at me with old, thin teeth.

"Shell got me, high explosive, blew my right foot off,"
the voice said pleasantly. "But the shell
had a tumble on it so it rounded the end of the bone."
A block away, the trees and benches of English Bay's promenade;
the blue ocean lying beyond in the early Spring sun.

"Those officers," the man said. "This one wanted us
to go up a hill to get some bricks for his safety-first dugout.
Our sergeant, he refused. It was already light, you see,
and the Germans could shoot at us there from three sides.

"But there were lots of officers like that. They were all over
England, strutting around." The man suddenly straightened, grinning,
put a swagger stick under one armpit and marched
important for an instant in the Army of another time.

"The bastards would come out as far as our third-line support trenches.
Then they could go back and wear a ribbon, here, 'returned soldier'
because they had been to France.

"This officer pulled his revolver out
and points it right at our sergeant. *Sergeant*, he says,
are you going to obey my order? So the sergeant
gets us together and says *I want you to go out single file
six yards apart. That way if a shell lands
you won't all be killed.* We made it to the farmhouse;
plenty of bricks there. Because I was the shortest
I was supposed to hold the bags open while the others shovelled.
Then the shell lands, and blows me over and over. The rest
made it into a little dugout about the distance to that car.
Bobby Johnston sticks his head out
and yells *Jess, Jess are you all right?*
They thought I was done for. *I'm okay Bobby*
I yell back, *but you keep down.* Then another shell lands

and two pieces of shrapnel catch him in the neck.
So there's the two of us lying out there. And my leg is
starting to hurt, like a toothache, but all over and much worse.
Shells are landing regularly, and I don't mind saying
I was shaking so badly I was vibrating like this
against the ground. They got out to me at last with a stretcher
but they had to drag it back to the dugout
crawling along the ground. The Germans could shoot at that hill
you see, from three sides. And they shelled us there
from seven to eleven-thirty, when I guess they had to stop
to cool their guns.

"Oh," he says, "I could tell you stories.
At the time, you know, they said we were fighting for Jesus Christ.
What a laugh. With the Pope and the Church of England
putting their money into armaments while we fought.
But I'm glad I lost the foot. I got my pension for it.
Otherwise, when I came back, I'd likely have been unemployed.
Before the war I'd been a sailor for a while on the Great Lakes
and done a little logging, and on the farm.
Afterwards, I was lucky to have that pension.

"Well, I could talk to you all day," he said
and turned, and began moving down the street again toward the water.

THE KUMSHEEN TRILOGY: 1. LYTTON

"Wayman," he said, calling me over.
"What do you think of the dance?"
And I sat beside him on one of the chairs
lining the walls of the community hall
while the rock band was taking a break.
He was a student I had met earlier that week
when I read my poems in the local high school.

"I don't do poems myself," he said. "But I do like to write.
I never have gotten on with my father
and sometimes when we have an argument
I get so damn mad I go into my room
and write: stories, anything, to keep from hitting him.
My sister writes poems, though. She keeps them in her room
and won't show them to anyone. She has some
about the time the school burned down.
When they had a display of photographs about the fire
I tried to get her to let me have a few
to go with the pictures, but she wouldn't."

The band crashes into life, and the hall stirs.
Mostly Indians are present, since the local ski club (all white)
is having its awards banquet this evening as well.
The young men dart in to stand in front of a seated girl
and nod, or touch her, and then the two
drift into the center of the noisy room and begin.

"Was I ever drunk last night," the student shouts at me
above the uproar. He is a white. "Four of us got five dozen
and sat on the grass behind the hotel.
I must have put away over a dozen myself.
By the end I couldn't even stand."

The music is too loud. We watch the dancers.
When they tested one class of grade nines and tens here last year
—Indians and whites—half did not know the name of this country.
And despite the strange colored cloth
flying on poles in front of the government buildings,
despite the presence of the federal police detachment

74

and the outline map behind the symbol of the television network
they could not explain what a nation is.

But all of them know this village
is where the Fraser River is joined by the Thompson.
And though there was no place on the paper to say it
the whites at least know they are not Indians.

Listening to the blasts of sound and the steady beat
from the band, I think about what anyone needs to know
and of the young man alone in his room in Lytton
moving his pen furiously to fill the lines of a page
to try to show a life to itself: words pouring out of a mind
that may not be able to define a country, or even say the name
of the one of which he and his words are supposed to be part.

2: SONG: I WISH I WAS AN EAGLE

I wish I was a canyon eagle
or one of the Lytton pines.
Because then this wind that always blows
wouldn't speak to me about bad times.

Two more are dead on the highway:
they didn't make the curve
just this side of Alexandra Lodge.
The police say they tried to swerve.

Forty-two cents for a sympathy card.
In the store I saw everyone stare.
Once at a Lytton Hall dance he said
I was the prettiest young girl there.

I took the card to his parents' house.
His mother was still drunk.
His step-dad didn't say a word.
He used to call him a punk.

Sometimes I sit up by the highway
and look out over the town.
Sometimes I sit at the canyon's edge
and watch the river flowing down.

Half this town hates the other half
all of the time, I think.
But whether you're Indian or whether you're white
there's nothing to do but drink.

I wish I was an eagle
or one of the Lytton pines.
Because then this wind that always blows
wouldn't speak to me about bad times.

3. SILENCE

Somebody lying passed out on the living-room floor
in the middle of the day is always a little awesome:
whoever it is, is probably not dead
but on the other hand you can't see the face
and so how old they are, or how big.
"Some mornings we get up," Jan says cheerfully
in the kitchen, "and there are four sprawled out in the front room.
I usually go from one to the other to see who they are."

These are usually Indians. They are known as the Thompson tribe
after the river named by the white explorers.
The Indians' own names are also
what the whites gave them: *Mary Billy, Johnny Jumbo, Billy Sam.*
A monument in the village commemorates the chief
who is credited with ending the troubles with the whites
that arose because, in the words of the plaque:
the Indians were using the land. For his peacekeeping efforts
he received from Queen Victoria a hunting knife and a medal.
Now much of the village depends on the reserve for money.
But there are still separate graveyards in use, and a Church
for each race.

On the floor the body twitches
lifts its black hair, and becomes Kenny.

He was drinking late last night, and when he went back
to where he stays—the house of the principal
of the Indian residence—the man had locked his doors
as he often does, to teach his boarders a lesson.
Many children whose parents have a house on the reserve here
have to live at the residence because of the drinking and fighting
     at home.
The young men also fight each other. The young women
take on five or six of the young men at once
in a kind of gang-rape and self-humiliation
that bothers even the men. One Sunday
Don found the body of a man on the railroad tracks
below the village, the face caked with dust.
He thought it was dead, but when he pulled at one arm

77

the man opened an eye for a moment, saw Don, and closed it.
"I got him up on my back," Don says, "and carried him up here
so at least he wouldn't be killed whan a train went by.
To me, the incident just about sums up this place."

And Kenny sits in the Sawyers' kitchen now
fingers shaking around a coffee cup
sipping occasionally and not saying a word as we talk.

LOOKING FOR OWLS

GARRISON

A man is running across Wyoming.
Away out on the high plains,
nothing around him but the wind and sky,
a man runs along the paved shoulder
of the great Interstate crossing Wyoming from west to east.
Cars pass him; the faces of children
stare out of rear windows.
And trucks pull by, the drivers high above the road
watch him run a long way ahead as they approach and go on.

Garrison is running across Wyoming.
He has always run. He ran in military school
and in the Army's summer camps.
"They wanted us to get up at 5:30 a.m.
So at 5 I'd be up doing laps. They couldn't believe it."
He went to college on a scholarship for track.
"I was good, but I wasn't that good.
I never could get into competition. I'd place,
but I think I only won in a meet once or twice.
I just liked to run. We'd have a good time,
me and a few others. I remember one relay
where the first guy on our team was great,
the second guy was good,
then they gave the baton to me.
I ran full out, but I lost most of the lead we had.
When I passed to my friend
he could see we weren't going to win:
he was even slower on that distance than I was.
So he ran one lap
then out of the stadium
into the dressing room
and was sitting outside having showered and changed
when the coach caught up to him.
The coach didn't know what to do.
He'd never seen anybody run right out of a race."

Now Garrison strides down a long hill in the afternoon sun,
his T-shirt plastered to his back, above the pavement,
face contorted with the strain.

"At college," he says,
"I used to run down from the jock dorm
about a mile to a little amusement park
where they had this miniature railroad
parents would take their kids on for rides.
There was a cinder track that paralleled the train tracks
so I'd run on that. Pretty soon
a train would come up behind
and I'd put on a burst of speed
to see if I could beat it.
The guy at the controls of the little engine
would open the throttle
nuh nuh nuh-nuh nuhnuhnuh and I'd tear ahead
trying to do better. People on board
would shout and wave
but I had to leap a couple of ditches
and in any case by the time I ever got to the park
I'd already run a ways so I wasn't exactly fresh.

"One day, though, I got into strip
and drove my car down.
I got out and hid in the bushes
on the further side of the worst ditch.
When the train came around the corner
I leaped out and yelled in the driver's ear
Let's go and took off up the track.
He opened her up *nuh nuh nuh-nuh nuhnuhnuh*
and took off after me, the people
screaming and cheering as he drew closer.
They thought they were helping win the race
but actually they were just sitting there yelling
and he would have gone faster if they weren't aboard.
Anyway, that time we were neck and neck
when we got round to the ditch again."

His feet, in Wyoming,
pull the asphalt behind him, stroke after stroke,
breath hauled in and pushed out with his long legs;
eyes blue under the blue sky.

He went to graduate school
in ROTC, studying education. He listened

82

to what people said about the War
and asked the Army about it,
so they let him go. After that,
he asked his professors about their work, too,
bringing his hound Ralph into classes
and offices, using the dog as a point of reference
in discussing teaching techniques.
He was living then at the edge of town
in a tiny cabin, and running
miles along the country roads
and laps around a tree-lined campus oval.

Until he quit, got a job working demolition,
then in the southern part of the state
went logging. "The only thing political down there,"
he says, "was the Birch Society meetings.
So I'd go along. Mostly it was a good place
to talk about hunting and trade guns and all that.
I'd refuse to take the oath of allegiance
to start the meeting. Freak 'em out.
Told them I was a Commie. Then we'd talk about dogs
and rifles. I kept winning most of the turkey shoots
they had down there, with my old single-shot.
They didn't know what to make of it. I figured
one crazy Commie at a Birch meeting
is better than a dozen films sent out from California.

"I remember one time I was over
talking guns with Billy Hankin.
I saw he had a couple of bumper stickers
on the back of his pickup:
Support Your Right To Bear Arms and
Support Your Local Police. 'Billy,' I said to him,
'you know if they pass a law outlawing guns
it isn't the Communists
who are going to come by to pick up your rifles.
It'll be Sheriff MacLeod.' Next time I saw the truck
the bumper sticker about the police was torn off."

He had enough education credits
to teach remedial subjects in the winters
and he logged, summers. He married

and got his teaching certificate finally,
had a daughter and hurt his back in the woods
so it had to be operated on.
Then his wife left him, and he came apart,
driving west to San Francisco non-stop
in his old jeep, and north into Canada
to a rural teaching job some friends got him.
There, too, he ran
and sat in the bar mourning his marriage
while the jukebox sang *you can't hide*
yer cheatin' eyes and he quit in January
and moved further north
to work as a counsellor on a ranch for delinquent boys.
"The kids could go to jail or to the ranch," he says.
"They were some mean little monsters.
A couple of them had been found guilty
of setting cars on fire. Shortly after they got to the ranch
they took off. We got the RCMP after them
and they were picked up in Hazelton.
The Mountie puts them into the back of his car
but one of them opens the door somehow
and zips away up the street. So the cop,
who isn't too bright, leaves one kid in the car
while he runs after the other.
By the time he gets back with the first kid,
sure enough, the other one had the cop car nicely ablaze.

"These kids are real puzzle-factory inmates,
penguins, that's what I call them. One night
a bunch of them got into a fight in the meal hall,
squirting ketchup at each other
and throwing bread around and everything.
I was supposed to be on duty, so I went in there
and didn't pay any attention to them
but began kicking over tables, smashing plates and cups,
tipping over chairs. Just went insane.
I looked up after a minute
and saw all the kids huddled into a corner
watching me. 'Now clean this up
and your mess too,' I said
and walked out, and they went to work
and got everything tidy. I just showed them

what it's like when an adult goes nutty.
No good yelling at them or threatening them.
They've had plenty of that.
If a penguin comes at me to hit me
sometimes I'll just wrap my arms around him
so he can't move his
and pick him up and dance with him. He gets really angry
but then he calms down and nobody gets hurt."

Now Garrison is travelling back to Colorado
for a long-delayed compensation hearing about his back.
"I never can do what I want to, Tom," he says
as we drive. "I got out of teaching because
I like to work with my hands. I have to stay in shape:
any job I've been on I want to work full out.
But most jobs, you're letting everybody else down
if you work too hard. I like the outdoor stuff at the ranch
but the place is crazy, it's really a jail,
the kids don't want to be there. And there's no women.
I go into town and meet somebody
and fall in love and make a fool of myself.
I don't want to do that. I want to be better to women.
But I don't know how."

His fingers reach up to twist
the thin blond hair above his forehead.
"Tom, who needs us? I mean
I think maybe this is the first time
people like us have been really useless.
What can we work at, give it everything,
that isn't hurting someone else
or adding to the sick way things are going?
What are we good for? Sometimes I honestly wish
I'd gone and fought in the War."

At a rest-stop, he says he wants to stretch,
cramped from riding in the small car.
He changes into strip and starts east down the freeway
while I finish some lunch, check the oil
and drive out after him.
A speck in the distance
at the edge of the highway

Garrison runs as the traffic speeds past him
in the hot day. The only human figure
in the vast panorama
of wind and landscape, a man
is headed for Rawlins,
running across Wyoming,
running towards Jerusalem.

THE CALF

"Fuck it," he said
as a light rain came up
where we sat being jolted and bounced
taking turns at the controls of the cat
breaking ground with a heavy plow behind:
"No more today."
So we climbed down
and ran for the car as the afternoon rain
hit and passed, while we drove to the house
between the fields of his father's cattle.

"Those cows there are mine," he said.
"I bought them with the money I got
working on the road crew last summer.
I run them with my dad's for now
but in a few years I should have enough
to sell some and buy my own quarter-section."
I asked him if a calf should lie like that
and he stopped the car. We got out.

The calf was on its side, all four legs
stretched against the earth.
As we approached,
it lifted its head to watch us
then suddenly rolled onto its stomach,
hoisted its back half
with its rear legs and tried
to push up with its front ones.
Part way up it stumbled, fell down, pushed again
and teetered upright, staring at us.
I stopped. Its left front leg
had no hoof, and the right leg, held above the ground
dangled brokenly below the knee.

Pat kept on. The calf
tried to get away: shifted its weight
to the raised leg, then
wrenched back in pain, lost its balance,
shuffled its legs frantically to stay upright
and then stood quiet

as Pat stopped too. "Shit," he said.
We looked at the calf
which stared back steadily.

"When that one was born," Pat said,
"its mother stepped on its hoof. Cows are really stupid.
It was winter, and the foot never did heal properly.
My father wanted to shoot it
but it's one of mine, so I had the vet
amputate the infected part.
It could get around on the stump.
It never weighed as much as the others
but it was coming along."

We turned back to the road. "What now?"
"No use talking to my dad.
He'd say butcher it for sure.
And the vet we got would agree.
That's what people around here are like:
if anything is out of the ordinary
they want to kill it.
I'll try to mend the break, I guess.
That way I'll get something for it in the fall."

He phoned from the house
but the vet refused to sell him material for a cast.
We drove into town, to the small local hospital
but they said no, too.
So we bought plaster of Paris at a hardware store,
then went over to the hotel for a drink.
"In this town," Pat said,
"once you've been away to the city
they figure you've burned your mind out on dope
and are crazy. My father
wants me to take over the farm so he can retire
but that would mean me taking on
about twenty thousand dollars in debts.
I'd work my whole life and never get free.
You know the story they tell
about the farmer who won a million dollars?
'What are you going to do with the prize?'
they asked him. 'Well,' he said,

'I plan to farm and farm and farm
until all the money is gone.' Fuck.
That's what it's like here.
I'd rather my dad just sold.
Of course, then I don't know what I'd do with my cows."
We ordered another round.

"They had this government guy
out from Regina, called a meeting
to talk about the government's new plan
which is supposed to make it easy
for young farmers to get started on the land.
The guy gave a speech
and then I stood up and showed him
how, even using his figures,
in five years you'd go broke. He hadn't allowed for interest,
for machinery, or anything."

                              We went back
and got Sandy, his wife,
and tore cloth into strips
and took rope and a pail of water and
drove out to the field. Again the calf
stumbled to its feet as we neared it.
I could see bone
sticking out of the fur of its raised front leg.

"We'll get it down," Pat said,
"and keep one foreleg lifted so it can't push itself up.
Once the cast is on
I'll tie it down overnight
to give the plaster time to harden."

He brought the shaky animal to the ground
and Sandy and I sat on it
while Pat, cursing, tried
to pull the damaged limb into position.
Suddenly the calf thrashed underneath me
like a huge fish, and I jumped off, scared.
It started to scramble up.
Despite its pain, its two bad legs,
the calf bucked and wriggled

but Pat was still on it
and fought the kicking, struggling beast alone.
He took a blow between his legs, got mad
and a second later had the calf down again
where he wanted it
and yelled for us to bring up the plaster and water.
We soaked strips of cloth in the mix
while he gently straightened the broken foreleg
and the bone slid inside.

We passed strips to Pat. As he worked
the calf watched us,
plaster dripping from the cloth
down onto its face near the eye. Pat held firm, though,
and when the strips were wound on
Sandy held the leg while Pat
roped the other legs together.
Then we went back to the house.
At midnight, we took a flashlight
and returned to look at the calf. It stared at us.
The next day, I was gone.

When I saw him
months later in Vancouver
he was back working as a welder.
I asked what happened with the broken leg.
"The cast was fine," he said. "I rigged up
some wire on the bottom so the calf could stand
without putting pressure right on the plaster.
A couple of weeks afterwards
just as the calf was starting to gain weight
one of my cousins drove by
and saw there was something funny about the animal.
So he shot it."

And Pat himself
the next winter, after the farm was sold,
sat in my room all one afternoon explaining
how he no longer needed to sleep
or eat.

Until they caught him

in a café up on Fourth. "I'm pretty bull-headed,"
he said later. "I was trying
to get the voices in my head to quit.
But I knew I had to be careful.
I figured if I ran at the wall at an angle
I could put myself out cold without snapping my neck."

THE WHITEWOOD ELEGIES

i A light, far off,
seen through a window of the house at night.

ii Sandy wrote: "On November 16
Pat committed suicide. He used
that stupid 8 mm. Mauser he bought in Vancouver,
if you remember. You know
he has been severely troubled; he has been in psychiatric centers
here in Saskatchewan and on medication, etc., at times
but he wasn't on any now.
He had come to live with me and the baby in Limerick,
then gone to the coast, when you last saw him,
and stayed with his folks who live on the Island now
and returned in the spring.
He was under care and seemed to be real good.
He got himself a job in Regina
which he held down right until the last.
He would phone me up and tell me he loved me, etc.,
and even come down, but
he was really tortured with his mind.

"He had just been down to see me that Sunday
and seemed to realize that he needed help again
but never made it. I was nice to him, thank God,
or I'd never be able to survive now. He is buried
in the churchyard near the farm, if you remember,
or perhaps he never took you there?"

iii Rage in the darkness
on the dirt roads
around Whitewood: 1972.
Pat at the wheel
as the tires churn through the summer dust
talking about his life
—his parents' farm again, and working maintenance
for the Highways, what he misses
of Vancouver, his few friends here.
Beside us on the seat, a bottle of rye,
"Saskatchewan acid" he calls it,

and we finally turn up the driveway of a farm
and stop under the sleeping house:

"Naw. They know me. They won't mind."

We open the whiskey, while the radio
brings in Winnipeg loud in the night
—rock and roll. "Quit worrying.
If they look out they'll recognize the car.
We can't drink on the roads
because what the Mountie does Saturday night
is drive around looking for people like us
killing a bottle in comfort.
That's crime in Whitewood
—that and using farm gas in your car.
Here we're okay; this is private property."

And later, through the windshield
a light travelling a distant road:

"Must be him. Nobody else would be out this way
at this hour."

We watch the light pass.

iv Now, driving in the late afternoon
   with a strong southwest wind
   and a white sky
   perhaps rain later.
   The utility poles
   head past, measuring the highway;
   the wide fields grown green
   the first June after his death.

   From the road, the land pulls back
   in slow, subtle hills
   of wheat, barley,
   flax, sunflower
   or the intense yellow of rapeseed.
   Trees stand in long groves on the horizons
   or close by the shoulder:

low poplar and birch scrub.

On the highway through Whitewood,
the Esso station that is also a restaurant
and the Greyhound stop
where Steve, coming from Vancouver one winter
to see Pat, unannounced and broke,
got off in the cold to phone the farm
and found him gone, working in the north.

The farm sold three years now, bought by a cousin.

And the wind along the road
pushing before it
the heads of the high green embankment grasses;
tall stalks
of yellow clover and wolf willow
nod again and again

It is his name
he gets remembered by—what it means
to whoever knew him,
and also the name of the land
of which he was one more
who drew in like a moving lamp:
a white man, a wagon,
a railroad, then the steady flow
of the highway traffic—another
of those planting the land
and paving it

with a name
and a light

v In the lounge of the Vancouver Island ferry
the next month, his head against the window,
coast sunshine
across the remembered, unexpected face.
He sleeps as the huge engines
heave the vessel forward through the Strait.

Perhaps in a moment he will awaken:

confused as always for an instant
then ready to laugh at himself for falling asleep
but bristly, too: staring round
in case anyone is mocking him.
Now his hands
lie in his lap:
the thick fingers, stained with nicotine,
placed there like ten familiar tools
ready to be picked up to get back to the job.

Beyond him
the steel deck
and the great fields of the sea
with their distant mountain rim.
An hour out of Tsawwassen, he sleeps
with his old Pontiac aboard
with the other vehicles,
his hair against the glass, and his face,
the face of a dead man
and the face of a stranger
soft and bathed now
in the whole light.

TRAVELLING COMPANIONS

At the bus station in Winnipeg,
buying a ticket for Winkler, Manitoba,
Wayman hears a familiar voice behind him:
"Make that two to Winkler." Wayman turns, and
it's Four Letter Word.
"I told you to stay back at the hotel,"
Wayman says. "I'll only be gone for a day.
It's a high school reading
and they asked me specifically not to bring you."
"Nonsense," Four Letter Word says,
reaching past Wayman to pay his portion of the fares.

"You're not welcome there," Wayman insists,
as he struggles out to the bus
with his suitcase and a big box of books to sell.
"That's not the point," Wayman's companion replies
as they hand their tickets to the driver
and climb up into the vehicle.
"Next you'll be ordered not to read
poems that mention smoking or drinking."

"I don't think you understand," Wayman begins
while the bus threads its way through the five o'clock traffic
and out onto the endless frozen prairie.
"The organizers of this program
asked me not to cause any trouble.
It seems somebody like you was brought into a school last year
and there were complaints all the way to the Minister of Education."

Four Letter Word stares out a window
at the darkening expanse of white snow.
"And you're the guy," he says at last,
"who's always telling people
I'm the one that gives the language its richness and vitality.
Didn't Wordsworth declare
poets should speak in the language of real men and women?" ·

"But it's a high school," Wayman tries to interject.
"Do you think the kids don't swear?" his friend asks.
"Or their parents? And I didn't want to bring this up,"

96

he continues, "but you depend on me. You use me for good reasons
and without me your performance will flop."
"No, it won't," Wayman says.
"It will," his companion asserts.
And the two ride through the deep winter night
in an unpleasant silence.

An hour later, they pull into the lights of Winkler
and here's the school librarian
waiting in the cold at the bus stop.
"You must be Wayman," he says
as Wayman steps down. "And is this a friend of yours?"
"I never saw him before in my life," Wayman responds
but his companion is already shaking hands with the librarian.
"So good to be here," he says, picking up Wayman's box of books.
"Now, when do we read?"

METRIC CONVERSION

Looking through his poems one day
Wayman suddenly stops, astonished. Just before a line
about driving 450 miles
a highway sign has been erected: two wooden posts painted green
and a thin metal rectangle which states *724 kilometers.*

Wayman flips ahead. Further on
in front of a mention of 300 pounds
another construction announces *136.36 kilograms.*
This sign is even fresher: the green paint
is still tacky when Wayman pokes it with his finger.

Wayman turns directly to a certain poem he remembers
and, sure enough, before a clause that reads
"the temperature was 40 degrees"
two wooden posts, unpainted, are stuck into the ground.
On a piece of metal leaning against them, Wayman sees
4 degrees Celsius. And nearby on the grass
two men are eating lunch
surrounded by their tools, cans of paint, lumber and sawhorses.

"What are you doing here?" Wayman asks. "Eating lunch,"
one of the men replies calmly.
"Listen," Wayman says, "I don't want your signs in my poems."
"Are these your poems?" the man asks, looking up.
"Yes," Wayman says. The two men stare at him, chewing thoughtfully.

"I want you to take your signs down and leave," Wayman resumes
after a pause. "It's all right, this is government,"
the younger of the two says. "In any case," the other man begins,
screwing the cap onto his thermos, "the way I view it is
we're doing you a big favor. Degrees Fahrenheit, ounces, yards
—who is going to remember what they meant in a few years?"
Both men have finished their lunches by now and are standing up.

"I don't want those things in my poems," Wayman persists.
"These terms make our ordinary world seem foreign, when it's not."
"Believe me," the older man says, as he and the other
prepare to hoist the metal signboard into place, "some day you'll
      be glad

we installed these. They might seem strange to you now
but without them pretty soon these poems would appear even
    stranger."

The two men lift the sign. "So instead of just complaining,"
the older man continues,
"could you reach into that toolbox
and pass us some of those five-centimeter nails?"

THE DEATH OF PABLO NERUDA

On the 11th of September, *his wife said,*

there was no sign of illness. It was his custom
to be up for the early morning news and then
after breakfast to read through the newspapers
before beginning work. In France
some days before Pablo received the Nobel Prize
he was operated on for his prostate
and during surgery they discovered the tumor was malignant.
But though he never knew this—the doctors
asked me not to tell him—it was felt
the cancer was contained and operable and he would live
many years. His own doctor, Roberto Vargas Salazar,
said he would live at least six years and probably die
of something besides cancer, as his was well controlled.

On the 11th he watched TV and heard the radio bulletins
all day. It hit him very hard. The next day
he woke up with a fever. I called the doctor in Santiago
—we were then living at Isla Negra—and he
ordered some injections. But the nurse who was to give them
could not get through to us. She lived in a village
only five or six miles away, but the soldiers
would not let her pass for two days.

His fever did not diminish. We tried to call
friends in Santiago to find out what was happening
but they had already been arrested or gone into hiding.
The doctor had said on the phone not to let Pablo
hear what was happening, but he had a radio
right by his bed and heard everything they reported
including President Allende's last broadcast.
Salvador was a great friend of his; sometimes at Isla Negra
he would arrive unexpectedly: there would be a great noise
and it would be the president's helicopter descending.
He would stay for supper and they would talk. Salvador was planning
a big celebration for Pablo's 70th birthday next July
with guests invited from all over the world. Pablo
was working at this time on six books of poems, simultaneously.

and his memoirs, which his publisher in Buenos Aires
intended to bring out on his birthday.

On the 18th, some friends were able to reach the house
who told him what took place in Santiago.
This was very bad for him. He was very ill in the evening
and the next day I called an ambulance to take him
to the clinic in Santiago. Because of the trouble the police made
it took quite a while for the ambulance to get to us.
As we approached the city, we found the police
were checking everyone. I told them
this was Pablo Neruda in the ambulance, who is very ill.
They acted as though they had not heard me.
They made me leave his side and I was checked. This
affected him very much. When I got back in
I saw there were tears in his eyes: it was the first time
in my life I saw Pablo cry. I told him
not to make so much of it, they were checking
everybody. All this time
I did not think he was really badly off
but that it was mostly the fever, which he had had before.
But Pablo was broken inside.

When we got to the clinic, the place was almost deserted.
Pablo's doctor had been arrested, but we got
another doctor. I learned that my house in Santiago
had been attacked by the soldiers and burned:
this happened while the government was saying
they would protect Neruda's property. On the 20th,
the ambassador of Mexico came to the clinic
and told Pablo that the Mexican president, Luis Echeverría,
was sending a plane to take him there.
Pablo refused to go. We tried to convince him
that he had to leave, but he still said no.
We went outside the room, and the ambassador
told me I should tell him about the house.
We went back inside and I explained we could no longer stay.
At last he agreed to go. I left him to go back to Isla Negra
to get some of our possessions, returning on the 22nd.
I discovered that while I was away, despite a guard at the door,
some people had been in and told him what happened
·· friends of his: all of this was very bad, Victor Jara,

one of his closest friends, was dead. Even our chauffeur,
who took no part in politics, was in jail
simply because he was our driver. That night

Pablo became delirious, crying out
"They are shooting them. They are shooting them."
I had the nurse give him an injection of tranquilizer
which I had in my purse. He slept
all night, and all the next day. At 10:30 at night
on the 23rd, while I was with him,
he had a convulsion and his heart stopped.
He passed from sleep to death; he did not suffer.

LOOKING FOR OWLS

Twenty miles from town, Michael had found
snowy owls living in the barn
of a farm with an abandoned house:
the farmer commuting from Saskatoon
to work his land. So we drove
one clear November afternoon
off the highway and along the back roads
by a pond with first ice on it.

At the farm, there was only the wind
and the sunlight. Tall grass
grew around the homestead
but a road still in use
led to the wide brown fields
turned over and left for the snows to cover.
Nothing in the barn. Michael said
a bull had been stabled there, but the stalls
were vacant, like the loft above:
no sign of the owls.

We went across and pushed open the door
to the farmhouse. The floor
was littered with the expected bits of glass
and brittle shards of linoleum.
In a place like this, Michael said,
a friend of his once found oak flooring under,
which the farmer let him have.
But not here, where there were only some rags
heaped in a corner of a closet. And outside,
the chill wind again.

                    But as we went
back along the fence
we saw a black mound in a field:
the remains of a bonfire
with unburnt planks protruding
from the heap of charred wood.
Not until we had walked out
and stood beside it
did we realize this was something else:

the nearest board
ended in a cloven hoof.
And past the other splayed legs
over its shoulder
we saw the head was missing.

Was this the bull Michael had seen in the barn?
But why kill it and set it on fire? Even a bull's hide
can be sold. And why cut off the head?
If it was vandals, why hadn't they just shot the beast
where it was in the barn? And if not,
why would anyone try to burn a carcass
in the middle of a plowed field
where what was left would have to be taken away
before planting next spring?

There were no footprints or tire tracks. Only the earth
running to a far line of trees on the horizon
and the wind along the furrows with nothing to say
about the scorched pile that had been an animal
beheaded and left in the November field
where the cold sky
stared down like the eye of an owl
that also wasn't there.

POEM COMPOSED IN ROGUE RIVER PARK, GRANTS
PASS, OREGON AFTER WAYMAN'S CAR STOPPED DEAD
ON THE OREGON COAST IN THE MIDDLE OF A
HOWLING RAINSTORM AND HAD TO BE TOWED FIRST
TO YACHATS, OREGON, WHERE IT COULDN'T BE
FIXED AND THEN ONE HUNDRED MILES THROUGH
THE MOUNTAINS TO EUGENE, WHERE AFTER IT WAS
REPAIRED AND WAYMAN STARTED OUT AGAIN HIS
ACCELERATOR CABLE PARTED AND HE HAD TO RUN
ON THE LAST DOZEN MILES OR SO INTO GRANTS
PASS AT MIDNIGHT WITH HIS THROTTLE JAMMED
OPEN AND SPEND THE NIGHT WAITING FOR THE
GARAGE TO OPEN WHICH IS AT THIS MOMENT
WORKING ON HIS CAR, OR RATHER WAITING FOR A
NEW PART TO BE SHIPPED DOWN FROM EUGENE
(AND WHICH GARAGE, INCIDENTALLY, WOULD FIX
THE CABLE BUT FAIL TO DISCOVER THAT ALL THAT
HIGH-REV RUNNING WOULD HAVE BLOWN THE
HEAD GASKET ON WAYMAN'S CAR CAUSING FRIGHT-
ENING OVER-HEATING PROBLEMS THE NEXT DAY
WHEN WAYMAN DID TRY TO BLAST ON DOWN TO
SAN FRANCISCO)

Let me not go anywhere.
Let me stay in Grants Pass, Oregon, forever.

GRANDMOTHER

In a house in Fresno, the television
lives with the family like a grandmother from the father's side.
She is up with the wife at six, when the baby daughter cries:
a grandmother willing to help, awake, but silent:
what she thinks flickers across her face without a sound.
While the father sleeps, the mother sits with the grandmother
feeding the baby: the eyes of the wife lift above the spoon
from the face of the child to the face of the silent grandmother.
The day outside begins to fill
with the sun of palmtrees; birds
call again and again from the high branches and leaves.

When the older child gets up, he stands at his doorway in pajamas
to stare at the familiar scene: his mother, grandmother
and the new baby. All day long in his play
in and out of the yard, the house, his meals and the steady sun
he goes back and forth by his grandmother
as she talks to herself, inwardly, her thoughts visible
but noiseless. In the afternoon, when the father wakes
the grandmother speaks to the older child for a while.
The parents glance toward her themselves now and then
as if to hear what she says. And once in the warm evening
the telephone says that the maternal grandmother
across the city is watching something on her own television
she thinks the child might like. All eyes
go on the grandmother, who begins talking again at once.
But the young body loses patience with the old
and she is left to address the empty California air.

Late at night, when the baby and the child are in bed
the parents gratefully turn to the grandmother.
When the mother goes on into the bedroom
the father listens to grandmother alone.
Then she is quiet, while he has his music
but her thoughts still pass restlessly across her face. At last
in the very early morning, the father says goodnight to the grandmother
and goes in himself to sleep. The grandmother sleeps,

the father sleeps, the mother sleeps, the little boy sleeps.
The baby turns fretfully in her crib, and cries out.
But there is no answer, and she sinks again, sighing,
back to her warm and milky infant's dream.

EGG CITY

"We have two million chickens," the manager said,
standing in the hot San Fernando Valley sun.
"We get three million eggs a day.
The chickens are housed in these buildings:
twenty thousand in each. We keep them
five to a cage, the maximum number
where they won't peck each other to death.
Inside the houses are parallel rows
of two cages back to back.
We monitor a single row
and if production falls below a set level
we kill all twenty thousand chickens
and replace them. We've found that's the most economical way
to run this business."

He led us to the door of one structure and we peered in
at the long noisy rows of wire mesh cages
packed with the constant white and red motion
of the thousands of birds.

"We have breeding farms further north,"
the manager said, "to supply us with new stock.
Feed comes from Texas on special barges.
We try to arrange other cargoes as well
so we don't have to pay for the barges to return empty.
And this is a machine we invented
to clean the floor under the cages:
the eggs are caught there, but the droppings
fall through the mesh to the floor.
This thing travels up and down the rows
and sweeps it in. We actually process the droppings
for any feed that might have passed right through the birds.
Then we bag what's left and sell it as fertilizer."

He took us into the rooms where the eggs
were being candled and packed. And, outside again,
showed us the distant corner of the ranch
where the day before they had all manned hoses
—management, the employees who commute,
and those who live on the premises—to fight off a huge brush fire

that had rolled to the edge of their fence.
But the manager was planning to resign in a few months
and emigrate to Israel, to a kibbutz specializing in poultry.
"This operation has grown so big,"
he told us, "I deal mostly in paper
and I never get to work with chickens any more."

But he returned after a year;
it hadn't been what he expected overseas.
And they gave him his former job back:
directing the sprawling, complex enterprise
whose entire output goes to provide
only a part
of the eggs Los Angeles eats every day.

THE HOUSE OF ST. DENNIS OF THE CHAMELEONS

i These suburbs
are filled with a great calm.

Palm trees rise over the lawns on a branchless stalk
and at last burst into green leaves high up in the warm air.

Jade bushes, ice plant and the green lime
grow in clumps between the street and the front door.

In these suburbs
it is always afternoon, or early evening.

ii Inside the houses
the air is cool.

Every counter or shelf
is empty: cleared of dust and clutter.

When a meal is eaten, the containers and plates
are quickly taken back into cupboards, and put away.

In the house an electric light
burns above a faded wall-to-wall carpet

burns clearly and steadily for hours.

iii In one room is a desk. On a corner
a stack of white paper, perfectly square.

A pencil lies on the desk-top, near the paper.
A typewriter sits in its case between a sofa and the wall.

When a word appears on the paper
the word is very still. It is as calm

as the room, as the house, the house
on Belladonna Street.

iv The word is *death*, on the paper
but nothing has died.

The word sits on the paper, very calm, very still
like a lizard, watching.

The word becomes the lizard, its eyes
are staring. The eyes of the lizard

watch the paper, the room.

v One edge of the paper
starts turning into sand.

TEETHING

In the dark house, the cry of a child.
Her teeth are trying to be born:
the tiny incisors
are cutting their way up
through flesh, into a mouth
now open and crying.

Deep snow around the house
beside the forest. Indoors, in the night
the sleepy voice of the mother, then the father,
and the child's steady crying.
All at once the father is up, and a moment later
he brings the child into another room
and sits in an old rocker.

The noise of the chair starts
as its wooden dowels and slats
adjust repeatedly to the weight being swung
back and forth. The chair moves
not with the easy pace
of someone assured, experienced,
but with the urgent drive of a young man
rocking and rocking. The chair creaks
persistently, determinedly,
like the sound of boots on the snowy road outside
in the day, going somewhere.

                    But it is here
the father has come to. In the dark room, in the chair
ten years as an adult pass, the chair
rocks out a decade of meetings, organizations, sit-ins.
It rocks out Chicago, and Cook County Jail.
It rocks out any means necessary
to end the War, fight racism, abolish the draft.
It rocks out grad school and marriage.
It rocks out Cambodia, and at last
jobs, a new country, and a child.

                    But the chair
          falls back each time

to the center of things, so it also rocks back
all these lives up into these lives: the father
rocking
with his child in his arms
at the edge of sleep. In the still house at Salmon Arm
the sound of the rocking chair
in the winter night. Sudden cry of the child.
Cry of the world.

WAYMAN IN LOVE

At last Wayman gets the girl into bed.
He is locked in one of those embraces
so passionate his left arm is asleep
when suddenly he is bumped in the back.
"Excuse me," a voice mutters, thick with German.
Wayman and the girl sit up astounded
as a furry gentleman in boots and a frock coat
climbs in under the covers.

"My name is Doktor Marx," the intruder announces
settling his neck comfortably on the pillow.
"I'm here to consider for you the cost of a kiss."
He pulls out a notepad. "Let's see now,
we have the price of the mattress, this room must be rented,
your time off work, groceries for two,
medical fees in case of accidents...."

"Look," Wayman says,
"couldn't we do this later?"
The philosopher sighs, and continues: "You are affected too, Miss.
If you are not working, you are going to resent
your dependent position. This will influence
I assure you, your most intimate moments...."

"Doctor, please," Wayman says. "All we want
is to be left alone."
But another beard, more nattily dressed,
is also getting into the bed.
There is a shifting and heaving of bodies
as everyone wriggles out room for themselves.
"I want you to meet a friend from Vienna,"
Marx says. "This is Doktor Freud."

The newcomer straightens his glasses,
peers at Wayman and the girl.
"I can see," he begins,
"that you two have problems...."

ANOTHER POEM ABOUT THE MADNESS OF WOMEN

It began as a joke: she did not like to leave the house
even to shop for groceries.
Now she wants to be better. On Saturdays
her husband and children drive her downtown
to one set of doors into a department store
and let her off: agitated, but resolved.
They drive around to the opposite side of the building
and wait.

What she has to do is push
between the people on the sidewalk into the store.
She must walk through the crowd, all the faces hurrying and stopping,
past the bright displays of merchandise, the cash registers,
until she reaches the doors that open into the other street.

Every Saturday. Until it becomes easier.
There were women in pioneer Iowa, too,
alone in the house all day
who saw from every summer window the corn around the house,
the tall green corn, high as a man, stretching away for miles
in the sunlight, swaying in the light breeze,
leaves rustling, whispering, heard
from the upstairs window in the dark, and the next day
whispering, until the woman knew
what stood on the ground everywhere, what surrounded the house
whispering and hissing
was alive, and hated her.

Here the electric clock in the kitchen runs
with hardly a hum. When she takes the garbage bags
out to the cans in the back lane she sees nothing but houses.

She knows there is a woman in each one.

D.: EIGHT POEMS
1. EXPLORATORY

Waking in the night, already in despair
I went deep into my body
and discovered
my heart, working away inside me
with its gigantic, noisy pumps
and machinery: tubes,
valves, catwalks, ladders, wiring
and dials, all busy,
and I understood for the first time
its tremendous indifference
like any machine: *what happens*
it says *in those outer few inches*
of flesh and skin and hair
that flatters itself
is a person
is nothing to me. My job
can be made more difficult
or easier
but I adjust if I can
and go on.

And watching it
function
according to a program,
a manual of operations
written long before I was born
and adopted before I could become aware,
it was clear
when my heart
or any room of the body
despite what I might want or need
gets its orders to stop,
it will stop. My heart

is working for someone else.

2. HOW QUIET

How quiet the words are.

Taken out of the swirl of a man's mind
while he sits in a room
moving a pen.

The noise of a car engine outside.
The starter turning over and over and over until the engine catches.

And then the click of a typewriter
and into an envelope and a metal box.
The factory sounds of the mail sorting.
Arrival at some publishers, talk
over the poems, and eventually

the racket of the printers: the drum of the presses
and the machines of the bindery
and more, sales and warehousing
and the retail trade.

Until the words sit under someone else's eyes
on a clean page.

Sit very still.

Even the reader fidgets, pulling his nose,
looking up at the door as he thinks he hears a noise in the hall

and then back to the perfectly motionless
printed letters

that are meant to refer to
the condition of being alive.

3. DISCOMFORT

Despite the terrible news, your illness
like everything else about living
contains its own discomforts:
the feel of an I.V. tube in each arm,
the bruises inside each elbow
where other tubes and injections have gone in
and blood taken out,
the small sores in your mouth that never heal
because the condition of your blood
means as simple an act as chewing irritates them.
So they put you on a soft diet:
the polite term for eating only applesauce and mush.

Plus feeling tired all the time.
And thus discouraged, even if nothing else
was present to discourage you: your voice on the telephone
weary and small, like a child
determined to be brave and yet sad at the same time.

And the endless frightening nosebleeds
(spontaneous hemorrhages to be exact)
each of which means calling a nurse
and a trip in a wheelchair to Emergency
to have the blood in the offending nostril suctioned out,
a local anaesthetic put in there,
followed by a swab of silver nitrate to cauterize it.
Finally, they stuff both nostrils with wadding.

And these events occurring in the middle of the night
so you can't sleep, and then the hospital routine
and your visitors—anxious, or already used to the situation—
making it difficult to get any rest during the day.
And there's the fever, present because the various treatments
have destroyed all your antibodies,
which has to be brought under control over a couple of days.
And waiting for the treatments themselves to have the desired effect
so the hospital part of this can be over for a while
and you can get out. And not thinking too much
of what it will be like in that indeterminate future
when you are back, that much closer to the end.

118

Understand, I'm talking about a young man, not even thirty.
There is a poem in here somewhere
of praise for the elderly
who after so much, a lifetime of discomforts,
are carefully moving a shopping cart
through a crowded food store: half pushing it
and half holding on to keep themselves up.
They, too, face these hospital unpleasantnesses,
clutching grimly and continually to their lives,
and are also making it—for a time—step by step.

But today, this is about Dennis
and what he endures.

4. TIDEWATER

2 p.m., June 28, 1976
North Vancouver Civil Court

They are fishing.
Dennis shuts off the outboard
and as the craft glides
into the small bay in the stillness,
Susan, in the bow,
reaches for a rock tied to a long cord
and lowers it over the side.
A light wind from the Strait
gently pushes the anchored boat
until its stern has swung round toward the shore.
In front of the green frieze of cedar and alder
Dennis bends over his tackle box
and fixes two rods. He passes one to Susan.
They sit waiting, with the lines out, in silence.
It is about eleven o'clock in the morning.

But under them the great tide is moving.
Across space, where by this day only a few men have travelled,
the invisible moon is turning around the earth.
It happens in this universe: one moon is held
by this planet, and the moon
pulls steadily back at the earth's salt water
on which Susan and Dennis are riding now.

A harsh series of clicks
from Dennis' reel: something has caught
what he offered; he begins to take in what lives
far down in the current.

As he does
Susan's rod begins dipping. She too winds in
and releases slack,
working against the tension,
so when the salmon breaks into the air for the first time
they can see it is tangled in both lines.
They reel in together, and let the fish run,
and haul in once more, until Susan

puts down her rod and picks up a small net
to lift the salmon from the water
and bring it dripping into the bottom of the boat.

They stare at it.
The fish heaves, and flops wildly,
then lies quiet, its gills gasping open and shut.
Dennis takes a small hatchet
and with the blunt end strikes
so that the fish flips and thrashes along the floorboards
again. After three blows,
the mad dancing
and the gills stop. A trace of blood
is in its mouth.

They look at what they have caught.
The salmon's sheen is fading
as its scales start to dry in the noon sun.
Dennis takes the oars and rows slowly in
to the beach. They unload the boat together
and while Susan builds a fire, Dennis
cleans the fish at the ocean's edge.
They wrap it in foil, and place it
in the hot ashes. They wait.

After an hour, they open the fire.
The flesh of the salmon is a rich red.
They share a container of salad they brought
and also some lemons, and wine.
As they eat
the tide is pulling the inlet toward them.
Dennis goes down once to check on the boat
but as he starts back up the beach he sees
a man standing at the fire.

Susan and Dennis are not afraid. They join hands
as the man speaks. *This is where you live,*
he says, *together,* and continues. Around them
they hear the green leaves lift and fall with his voice
while behind them is the water
married to the moon.

5. FIGURING

Horsetail ferns suddenly growing this Spring
in the vacant lots,
the unruly hedges between the back yards
a mass of yellow light and shadows,
and I ask myself
what must it be like for you to look at something
—perhaps the new chestnut leaves
shading the still-cool avenues—
and think: *this might be the last time
I get to see that.*

I begin to understand those people
who spread the gloomiest possible stories about you,
who seem to just want it over
like a fatal heart attack.
But random chance, we're learning,
doesn't always mean finished
but rather a continuing difference
from what might have been expected.

In my case, fury begins:
it's like someone is bullying you,
as if you were walking along the street
and got slapped around for no reason.
Or you were driving home one afternoon
when a drunk runs a red light
and smacks into the side of your car.
He's unhurt and sorry about it the next day
but his insurance pays for the damage
and he continues on with his life
while you have to stay in the hospital for years
or never do recover.

Of course it's all random:
that you became what you are
and that you could go on to do more
or that this happens—I want to show you a list
I made, of the range of possibilities,
how you accomplished so much by this year
by chance, too, in a way,

because, as with everybody,
if this and this hadn't happened
or had
things would have worked out differently.
It's the same chance
that lets us get born in the first place
and begin that collection of accidents, defeats,
achievements and neutral events
we call a life.

I decide it's like reading a book:
every time is the first time and the last time.
Even if we pick it up for a second reading
it's another experience entirely than the first.
So with this Spring. And we're at peace:
it isn't hard to imagine
how horrible war is
to cause anything like your situation
to happen to one other person....

Yet none of this calculation
is much comfort,
really.

6. FAREWELL TO WHEELER WITHOUT SAYING GOODBYE

after Eduardo Escobar

We were always envious of you, Dennis Wheeler,
envious and admiring and proud, too,
of how without seeming to make any unusual effort
you moved right to the front of whatever was happening.
For example? Disappearing that summer in the university
to work in the Arizona desert with Solari
before the rest of us, your friends,
realized there was such a thing as architecture.

When some of us began to be interested in poetry
you had already been to San Francisco
and met Ginsberg and Creeley. Jack Spicer
had dedicated a poem to you
prior to us even knowing there was a problem
about what constitutes a line.
And by the time Charles Olson became one of the deities
locally worshipped from afar
you were down in the Yucatan on a grant
observing the correspondences between
Mayan and Northwest Coast Indian art.

No wonder we hated you. And were awed:
to visit your place was to see on the shelves
at least fifty books we'd been meaning to read
and to have you show us
another twenty-five we then felt we should.
Also, there were the dozens of pamphlets,
magazines, manifestoes and poems lying around
we were certain we ought to be taking notes about
and be prepared to discuss forever.

Yet when we left you, having borrowed at most three books
—all we could admit to needing right now
and planning not to return these—
what was worse was knowing you were somebody
exactly like us: a kid from New Westminster our own age
or, in my case, a couple of years younger,

someone who had worked in the mills
to get money for school like anybody else
and whose father was no more and no less than a good carpenter
—one of those contractors with one steady employee
who after ten years of work together is also his best friend
and to whom he finally offers a partnership in the business
but the other man refuses, saying:
You're the boss. You keep the worries.
And they argue about that for the next ten years while they hammer.

You became immersed in the visual arts, Dennis,
and flourished there, writing reviews and travelling
from the coast to New York, absorbing so much
none of us could understand what you wrote
and so used to laugh at you whenever we got together
and then had to sneak off one by one
to ask you to explain what you were doing.
Eventually, even the government
acknowledged your achievements
and appointed you western liaison officer
for the National Gallery, with an office in Vancouver
that had an eight foot high geodesic dome
inside the door, various schemes underway,
and prints and papers on the walls
and falling from the desks, file cabinets, tables and chairs.
About this time, though, the art world
commenced to rub beards with Marx
and at last this was something
the rest of us thought we already knew about
—in another context, however, namely the street.
But no, you still had access
to ideas and books we had never heard of
and once again we were visiting you
and borrowing and reading and talking
as fast as we could to keep up.
Then the word was: Marx or no Marx,
the visual arts had dead-ended. Okay: you were off
making films, and not just any movie
but a film about Indians, now that Wounded Knee
and cinema and radical aesthetics
were precisely what was important,

at least in those worlds that take count of such things.
Naturally, the first film you work on
is a huge success. Everyone says so,
including the *Village Voice* and the *New York Times,*
both of which are a long way
from your basement suite at 2202 B Cypress Street,
if you know what I mean.
And of course there is local praise
and approving nods from Toronto.

But at this hour, with each of us
left gnashing our teeth and open-mouthed with wonder
—at the same time, which is no easy feat in itself,
while you are working away on other films,
some nearly finished and some
growing in your mind and on paper,
just at the instant when there starts to be
a rush of books and lectures and discussions about
dying and death,
comes this.

You always were first.
And now you've pulled ahead of us again.
So you won't mind if I don't say goodbye.
What's the point? The rest of us
will be catching you soon enough.
Once more you proceed to show your friends
so much we never thought of
for the rest of our lives.

And yet, maybe this time
we'll have enough distance
to add to our resentment of you—
memory, which perhaps can alter
everything we ever thought or said
or think and say about you,
can change these most complicated of emotions,
and transform the examples you set us, what we learned
and in fact all our recollections

into pure love.

7. LA LLUVIA DE TU MUERTE

He died on a rainy Tuesday in the autumn
and the rain washed him away.

He died in Vancouver, our City, in the morning
and the rain washed him away.

The rain washed away his face, the face of a brother.
The rain washed away what a face feels
as the drops of rain strike it
on a street, in Vancouver,
and the rain washed him away.

It took his name, the name of my friend,
and left only the letters of his name.
It took the way he walked
and what he did Saturday afternoons.
It took art galleries, used furniture stores, libraries;
it took Kitsilano Beach.
It took everything he ever saw
and it washed him away.

He died with thunder in his mind:
thunder without sound
but with each flash of lightning so white and sudden
his ears rang continually.
He died of cancer, which in thirty years
may be as preventable as polio is now.
But in this time, in these thirty years, cancer killed him at thirty.

After thirty, men's faces begin to fatten.
After thirty, it begins to be obvious
many people will never amount to much.
After thirty is late to marry, late to begin a family.
Even so, he died at thirty
and the rain washed him away.

When a great pain fills the body
what you are leaves
so all that remains of you is the shell of the pain

and an enormous fear.
He died in pain.
But he lived in a quick wit, intricate, subtle,
and what he thought he passed on to those around him.
Like every friend, he taught me, and like no other
this one taught me some ways to think about writing, about art.
He taught some people about rain, but not me.
He died in the rain.

He died in the rain and the world got smaller
for me, because when he was alive he was a brother
and when he died, a brother.
He was alive, and he died, and there is still the struggle.
And a shadow where he was, and the rain.

8. AN EPITAPH: D.W.

Three o'clock. A February afternoon
about eight degrees, windy and very clear.
From the top of the East End
on Nootka Street
the sweep of the North Shore mountains: Grouse, Seymour,
Coquitlam, new snow on them
lower than before. On this side of the inlet
to the north and east,
the hills studded with roofs and buildings of the City:
Vancouver Heights, Capitol Hill, and then
the treed park of Burnaby Mountain.
Far to the east and south
the ranges of the Cascades show pure white in a distant sunlight:
Mt. Baker rising in the southeast with its attendant peaks and clouds.

And here
the City: a trail of litter along the sidewalk
up Second Avenue from Renfrew
from the corner grocery to the paperboys' shack
and beyond: Smarties boxes, bags from McDonald's hamburgers,
the bottom half of a container of Dairyland sour cream
plus dozens of other, indistinguishable shreds and bits of paper.
Sounds of the wind, and the traffic on the main roads.
No one in the street.

WHAT GOOD POEMS ARE FOR

To sit on a shelf in the cabin across the lake
where the young man and the young woman
have come to live—there are only a few books
in this dwelling, and one of them
is this book of poems.

                    To be like plants
on a sunlit windowsill
of a city apartment—all the hours of care
that go into them, the tending and watering,
and yet to the casual eye they are just present
—a brief moment of enjoyment.
Only those who work on the plant
know how slowly it grows
and changes, almost dies from its own causes
or neglect, or how other plants
can be started from this one
and used elsewhere in the house
or given to friends.
But everyone notices the absence of plants
in a residence
even those who don't have plants themselves.

There is also (though this is more rare)
Bob Smith's story about the man in the bar up north,
a man in his 50s, taking a poem from a new book Bob showed him
around from table to table, reading it aloud
to each group of drinkers because, he kept saying,
the poem was about work he did, what he knew about,
written by somebody like himself.
But where could he take it
except from table to table, past the *Fuck offs*
and the *Hey, that's pretty good*s? Over the noise
of the jukebox and the bar's TV,
past the silence of the lake,
a person is speaking
in a world full of people talking.
Out of all that is said, these particular words
put down roots in someone's mind
so that he or she like to have them here—

130

these words no one was paid to write
that live with us for a while
in a small container
on the ledge where the light enters

NOTES

1. "The Unemployment Insurance Commission Poems: 2. A Cursing Poem": "Manpower" here refers to Canada Manpower, a government agency. To qualify for unemployment insurance, an applicant must register with Manpower as looking for work.

2. "Neil Watt's Poem": One of our partsmen used to cope with his job by pretending the material we worked with was alive — for example, complaining loudly if he saw me drilling holes in a fiberglass hood shell. I liked his idea, so I call this poem after him.

3. "Bob Kine's Song": On any job, there's always a guy who can't stay out of trouble. This friend at work who is one of those used to hum a blues refrain I liked. Finally I stole the refrain to use in this poem.

4. "Cumberland Graveyard, February 1973": I became fascinated for a while with the story of an early Vancouver Island coalminer, Ginger Goodwin. Goodwin was one of the miners arrested when the Canadian Army occupied the Island coal districts to break a strike just before the First World War. During the war, Goodwin rose in the trade union movement at Trail, B.C., but at the height of a strike he was leading he was drafted. He fled back to the Island coal districts to hide out, but some months later was shot and killed in the bush by a special policeman. The day he was buried the first B.C. general strike was held to protest his murder.

5. "The Blue Hour": Sometimes in Vancouver, where I live, in the long evenings of early summer the air just before dark turns a certain shade of blue. When this happens, it seems every object in the City takes on the same color, the same shade.

6. "Friends Logging": B.C. coastal logging uses a system of overhead cables to pull or "yard" out of the bush trees previously cut by fallers. A chokerman attaches a cable to the log, and at a signal the logs are yarded in to a central point and stacked in a pile known as a "cold deck," ready for loading onto trucks.

7. "The Kumsheen Trilogy": These poems are about a village in the Fraser Canyon about 150 miles from Vancouver. I got to know the place a little because friends of mine taught school there for two years, and I visited a number of times.

8. "D.: Eight Poems": In the spring of 1975, a Vancouver friend, Dennis Wheeler, was diagnosed as having leukemia. Those of us who knew him had to attempt to come to grips with a person who for a long time was very much

alive, but also seriously ill. His sickness went through stages when things were very bad, and other periods when it looked like a normal life might be possible again. He was ill for two and a half years.